SO MUCH THINGS TO SAY

Photo © 2010 Cookie Kinkead

Over 100 Poets From the First Ten Years
of the Calabash International Literary Festival

Edited by
KWAME DAWES & COLIN CHANNER

Published by Akashic Books
©2010 Calabash International Literary Trust
Managing Editor: Justine Henzell

ISBN-13: 978-1-936070-07-7
Library of Congress Control Number: 2009910813
All rights reserved

First printing

Akashic Books
PO Box 1456
New York, NY 10009
info@akashicbooks.com
www.akashicbooks.com

Printed in Canada

TABLE OF CONTENTS

There Are Places Where the Spirit Breathes: Calabash!

I must have been fifteen, perhaps sixteen. I was assigned to write an essay, "une dissertation" as it was called back then in Belgium, on a single poignant sentence written in 1913 by Maurice Barrès: "There are places where the spirit breathes." ("Il est des lieux où souffle l'esprit.") Later on, I learned more about this writer's questionable political leanings, but for me this sentiment remains pure.

I do not remember what I wrote back then. I would like to remember what place or places I chose to illustrate this sentence. Today, I elect Calabash.

For the past ten years of our new millennium, in late May, more than two thousand people have come every year to Treasure Beach, Jamaica, to the Calabash International Literary Festival, to talk and listen to writers, artists, poets, travelers from around the world. Those who come to listen do so under a tent on the beach with nothing but the waves as a backdrop; those who come to talk or hold a public conversation or read poetry do so in front of an audience that is different from any I have ever encountered. The quality of attention is deeply engaged, joyous, celebratory.

I was there in May 2009, sharing the stage with Pico Iyer, the great travel writer who is, more accurately, one of the great writers about place. The subject we chose to pay attention to and digress upon was simple: what does it mean to come from somewhere? We spoke of George Santayana's 1912 essay "The Philosophy of Travel." Santayana writes that "The roots of vegetables (which Aristotle says are their mouths) attach them fatally to the ground, and they are condemned like leeches to suck up whatever sustenance may flow to them at the particular spot where they happen to be stuck." He goes on quite naturally to contrast the vegetable kingdom, its placidity and inability to "make a chance acquaintance," with the "privilege of animals," that is locomotion, which is "perhaps the key to intelligence." They owe that intelligence, Santayana believes, "to their feet."

Hardly immobile, the audience of several thousand was in agreement, their bodies in movement, responding vocally; it was thrilling, a connection neither Pico nor I had ever felt before anywhere with any audience. We were not just having a public conversation, we were partaking in a ritual, a form of cognitive theater—what listening together should be, and which it rarely is.

Isabel Allende has said that in South America you make love first through the ears. The ear is a delicate organ. What we hear has the power to transform us, deeply. The Greeks already knew this, and Plutarch among them believed that *listening* is at once the most *pathetikos* (passive) and the most *logikos* of senses; as Michel Foucault reminds us, the ear can receive the *logos* better than any other sense.

To the passive side of listening, Foucault quotes Plutarch: "We cannot avoid hearing what takes place around us. After all, we can refuse to look; we close our eyes. We can refuse to touch something. We can refuse to taste something." But remember even Ulysses could not escape the Sirens, and had to block his ears to not fall victim and become "bewitched by their songs and their music."

To the active side of listening, Foucault writes: "We do not learn virtue by looking. It is and can only be learned through the ear: because virtue cannot be separated from *logos*, that is to say from rational language, from language really present, expressed and articulated verbally in sounds and rationally by reason. The *logos* can only penetrate through the ear and thanks to the sense of hearing. The only access to the soul for the *logos*, therefore, is through the ear."

I am convinced that when Kwame Dawes, Colin Channer, and Justine Henzell dreamed up the magic of holding an annual literary festival in Jamaica, on Treasure Beach, they intuitively had in mind a festival where the compelling double nature of listening as both receptive and active would be present and celebrated.

Last year, as I sat with Sam, my seven-year-old son, in the audience, we listened to Robert Pinsky declaim his poetry to an enraptured audience. His words, in this setting of heightened receptivity, entered deeply into our souls and minds. The involvement was present again, as was the acknowledgment that something special was happening to us, while congregated to hear this poetic sermon on the beach. It is fitting and just that one hundred poets be brought together in this beautiful anthology, *So Much Things to Say,* to celebrate the tenth anniversary of Calabash, a place where the spirit breathes deeply.

Paul Holdengräber is the Director of Public Programs—LIVE from the NYPL—for the Research Libraries of the New York Public Library

Oh, when the rain fall,
It don't fall on one man's housetop.
Remember that . . .
—Bob Marley, *"So Much Things to Say"*

Imagine a night of a hundred poets reading their work to an audience of intensely engaged, responsive, and lively people — say three thousand of them. They are a loud bunch when it is time to make noise, but they are silent as congregants at prayer when the poets' language entrances them. Imagine the reading taking place under a tent pitched on a grassy lawn that overlooks the Caribbean Sea. Imagine that this is not the north coast of Jamaica, with its cliché of white sands and coconut trees, a place glutted with cruise ship passengers and bewildered tourists; imagine instead a rugged coastline, a landscape full of the kind of character we find in the weather-beaten faces of wise old folk; imagine fishermen, farmers, ordinary workers, schoolchildren, and traveling people moving around as if they have been in this place forever and as if they all belong. Imagine the sun setting, imagine the scent of curried goat and frying fish wafting through the air; imagine the heat, imagine the cool tongue of wind off the sea; imagine a stage like an ancient shrine with a podium artfully pieced together with bamboo, strips of still-green wood, leaves, twine, and shells. Imagine one hundred poets, some whose names you know and some you have never heard of, stepping onto the stage, opening their mouths and hearts, and singing out poems of great variety, complexity, beauty, and passion. At once you are in a timeless place in which the spoken word represents an incantatory ritual that creates and affirms community, and yet you are in a deeply modern world where people are contending with wars, computers, airplanes, and the rapid nature of communication—people from all over the globe are connected in this moment and strangers rapidly become familiar, almost friends in an instant. Imagine laughter and tears, imagine sighs of familiarity and moans of pain, imagine tragedies enacted in the words that move through the shelter of the tent; imagine a poem like a fist, or a sharply painful open palm, or the tender caress of fingers, or the firm grasp of a handshake. Imagine stories dropping like seeds into the ground and growing rapidly and wildly all around you.

This is what a poetry reading at the Calabash International Literary Festival is like, and this event has welcomed a wide range of poets over ten years, who, when listed together, represent at least one reckoning of the place of contemporary poetry in 2010. Poets from across the world, some with awards in their satchels, some with fancy imprints under their names, others with the pure joy of seeing their work in a published book, still others with just their words to share; all of them gathering as if to speak for the first time; all of them stepping to the mic and sharing their work with power and grace. Usually, by Sunday evening, the festival which starts on a Friday night is over for the year. It will take another eleven months of planning, inviting, and reimagining the festival to bring it to life again.

In this new anthology, however, readers get a taste of what the festival offers year after year, and it does so in two ways: It features poets who have read at Calabash, some seventy-five of them, over nine years. It also features the work of up-and-coming Jamaican poets who are fellows of the Calabash Writer's Workshops that take place in Jamaica year-round. *So Much Things to Say* is an exciting example of Calabash's commitment to its core aims: to create a festival that is diverse, inspirational, earthy, and daring; and to offer a free literary event of the highest quality in Jamaica each May. This anthology is at once a celebration of ten years of a remarkable festival, a gesture of love, and a vehicle to fund and support Calabash for the future.

Like everything Calabash, this anthology is quixotic. As were the intentions of me and fellow Jamaican author Colin Channer, traveling together on trains through London some time in the late 1990s, singing every '70s reggae tune that we knew and conspiring to create a literary festival that we would want to attend every year; this anthology comes from that same spirit. Here we have an anthology that true Calabash folks will want to read. Poetry, it is said, does not sell. To think that an anthology of poems might help to support the Calabash Festival is absurd. But everything about Calabash is at first glance absurd. And yet this madness has proven to be a lasting success.

When Justine Henzell and I started to contact the poets who have read at Calabash to see if they would donate a poem, we expected the task to be daunting and time-consuming. But in the space of a month, all the poets had consented and most had already submitted work. The response was classic Calabash. They answered the call with joy, excitement, and with not a hint of hesitation. They sent us beautiful poems. Some sent fresh poems, never before published; some sent poems that have become familiar anthems; some sent poems about Calabash; some sent poems about what they saw outside their window that day. Yet they all sent poems and they all gave us permission to include their work in this volume.

So Much Things to Say is organized in the way that we imagine people often read anthologies of poetry. We imagine that people wake up in the morning and think, *I could use a really short poem today.* Or they might be walking home after work and say, *Man, I feel like reading an epic when I get home tonight.* Colin Channer imagined, also, that few people read a collection of poems from front to back in one sitting. Instead, he surmised, we often dip in and select poems depending on how much time we have to take the plunge. Well, we have made it easier for you. In the spirit of individuality and a resistance to the idea of "one size fits all," this anthology is organized by size—not by the size of the authors themselves, or the size of their imaginations, but by the size of their poems.

If you are holding this book in your hand, and if you actually bought it, then what you are doing is supporting the work of the Calabash International Literary Festival and ensuring its survival for years to come.

If you think this book is beautiful, then you must remember that Akashic Books, who agreed to partner with Calabash in making it happen, is the hippest and most forward-thinking press around. If you are seduced by the photos scattered throughout this anthology, then you must know that these images, too, were donated to us by a wonderful set of "Bashical" photographers—Ian Cumming, Cookie Kinkead, Jonathan Orenstein, and Sally Henzell—who have long been a part of the festival and what it represents.

All profits from this publication will go toward the running of the festival, which remains free and open to the public. Most importantly, however, this book is a treasure trove of poetry by writers who have come to love this festival and what it stands for. Anyone interested in a taste of where international poetry is today will have a chance to experience it in this dynamic and unusual anthology. Beyond that, *So Much Things to Say* is the closest thing that you will get to actually sitting under that tent among thousands of people who understand themselves to be as much a part of the drama of the reading as the poet standing at the podium.

Imagine that it is dusk. Imagine a white mongrel slipping into the shadows under an almond tree. Imagine seeing a specter of white moving slowly toward you. Imagine that as the specter comes closer you realize it is letting you know where the path is. Imagine yourself stepping through the dark as this specter becomes a human figure. Imagine that when you are close enough you can see a shock of long white hair, a world-worn face of wrinkles, eyes of sparkle and blue, a long beard, the white of a too-large shirt. Imagine a grin so welcoming and luminous that it makes you grin back. Imagine that this man speaks softly with laughter in his voice in a polished Jamaican accent. "Hey, how you do?"

And imagine your reply as he moves right by you smelling of good herb and the sea. "Good, Mass Perry, doing good. How you do, sah?"

"Just fine, man, just fine."

Kwame Dawes
Columbia, South Carolina
April 2010

PART I: SMALL

Photo © 2003 Jonathan Orenstein

Tikki-Tikki

hungry chickens
in a coop

water spilling
from a busted pipe

the bass of the music
played a haunting rhythm

in her stomach
if this was how it had to be

she would recline
massage her lower abdomen

knead oil into her limbs
then go among them

a breeze they welcome
in the heat of the day

On my desk is a photograph of you
taken by the woman who loved you then.

In some photos her shadow falls
in the foreground. In this one,
her body is not that far from yours.

Did you hold your head that way
because she loved it?

She is not invisible, not
my enemy,
nor even the past.
I think
I love the things she loved.

Of all your old photographs, I wanted
this one for its becoming. I think
you were starting
to turn your head a little,
your eyes looking slightly to the side.

Was this the beginning of leaving?

You chose to leave; that's fine by me.
"One's country," John Milton said, "is wherever
it is well with one." You're still my friend.
Is true, poor people catching hell
and the middle class sleeping
with panic button under their pillow;
but when you fly down to visit
and enjoying the old veranda lime
after dinner, don't spend the time
trying so hard to get me to say
you did right, only a loser would stay.
I wouldn't say I would never leave,
but if that's what they call ambition,
then right now I sticking with love.
River mullet still running in Grandy water,
and the busu soup simmering, keeping warm till you come.

He tells me to climb on the wall outside.

I'm sweating so hard it looks like I showered in my uniform.

His instructions are simple:

Don't come down until you blow out the sun.

I look up and blow.

It looks like I am whistling to God.

Native kling-klings, singed again
by migrating white cattle egrets
and brutal sun

have chickened to ground
and strutted and molted
to chattering
blackbirds
jostling for quick bread.

Unflappable
in V formation,
the egrets wing at evening
to feather communal nests

while ruffled by another
day of poor pickings
in a resort
to hawking
for crumbs from the tourist's palm
the brooding
black
birds
are
coming
home to roost.

Natalie G.S. Corthésy

Five-fingered pendulum
swing, the promise kept.
A guillotine descent
from queen to dutty bitch.
And so it is I was even asked
to return the ring.
Willing myself to remain equidistant
from the marriage that consumed our illusions
and replaced them with parodies
interlocked like safety pins,
I began the ritual of convincing myself
that I was not spit in the soup.
Sun licks sky with liquored lips
overlooking the restless city
slowly come to a halt.
With feathered hand
I left the door
ajar with thoughts of I, you, me,
will we cease to we-arise from now on.

Calabash Writer's Workshop Fellow

Marsha-Jay Dallas

When I was younger
she would beat me.
Now, we argue
fearing reality.
Then, spent
we wait
knowing
that tomorrow always comes.

Wondering when time
would heal itself
I held onto her arm and cried.
Then, biting her lips as always
she pressed my haunting face
close to her chest.

Calabash Writer's Workshop Fellow

Ever so often
the wind comes
with heightened sounds of your pain
and fragrances of cedar
like the scent of new wood
prepared for the parting.

It's a rural thing,
any minute now
I expect to smell the rum.
Hum hum hum hum hum hum hum
Hum hum hum hum hum hum hum

life my dear
will acquire injury

bruises happen incidentally
the toothless bite tender
and caress do also cut

oh there are people my dear and plants

you warm them
between your hands
for all hurts and sources
contact to balm

these are wonders
of the world dear
and if you plant
them all will grow

I don't care what you say,
fish is for eating
not for dreaming.
I made a pillow covered in ducks once,
but I never finished it.
I just left the pins in
and all the stuffing came out.
Oh well, I guess duckies aren't my *thing*.
But the orange glow from a sleep button
really makes me tingle.
I am a woman,
because I bleed like one,
I'm moody like one
and I've got that look between my legs.
Anything past that point is standard.
People don't do standard anymore.
Dollies are proof of that.
So I'm going say it one more time—real loud unlike a lady,
I'M KEEPING MY MILK!

Calabash Writer's Workshop Fellow

many flowers have met untimely
deaths at the hands of the lovelorn
during attempts to ascertain
in a most unscientific way whether
he loves or he does not
the thread of thought curves round
income statements and balance sheets
to a poem about the rain in Ireland
that due to a clever line break takes you, in
a word, from illicit images to the mundane
walking home from grocery shopping
with someone you love in the rain . . .

Calabash Writer's Workshop Fellow

Soldiers with guns are at our door again.
Sister, quick. Change into a penny.
I'll fold you in a handkerchief,
put you in my pocket
and jump inside a sack,
one of the uncooked rice.

Brother, hurry. Turn yourself
into one of our mother's dolls
on the living room shelf. I'll be the dust
settling on your eyelids.

The ones wearing wings are in the yard.
The ones wearing lightning are in the house.
The ones wearing stars and carrying knives
are dividing our futures among them.

Don't answer when they call to us in the voice of Nanny.
Don't listen when they promise sugar.
Don't come out until evening,
or when you hear our mother weeping to herself.

If only I could become the mirror in her purse,
I'd never come back until the end of time.

in the kitchen in the hills
the man strains pasta
the cloud of steam shrinks him
back to child
back to the kitchen on the flats
to mama pouring the long long
line of steaming chocolate
from cup to cup
to cool in the early
school
day morning

As I watched the sea
tossing its arguments
at the silent shore

the wind blew an almond leaf
at my feet.
I asked it for its message.

"My days on the tree are done,"
it said.
"There is no going back in this form.

Now yellow and brown with age
I am sinking back to the soil
whence my cycles

will be as mysterious and long
as the sea's reasonings
with the land."

Kei Miller

If this short poem stretches beyond
its first line, then already, already,
it has failed, become something else,
something its author did not intend
for it to become, a misbehaving,
rambunctious, own-way thing,
its circuitous journey a secret known
only to itself, its tongue its own.
The author is destined, I am afraid,
to write poems that escape him.
This, for instance, was to be just one
line long, or even one long line,
dedicated to Mervyn Morris and his love
for brevity; but it has become something else
entirely. The poem sings its own song,
reaches its own end in its own time.

Grandma, much younger
than her age-paper,
is giggling on the floor
with baby Jon
as with his daddy
forty years ago. "Age
is just a number,"
as the slogan says.

Grandpa, seeming
buried in a book,
gives thanks for her
endearing gift
and mumbles Larkin,
"What will survive of us
is love."

SUNSHINE

woke up
this mornin'
kissed
the sun
told her
good mornin'
there's work
to be done
so shine
sunshine
shine
in my life
today
shine
bright light
burn clouds
away
let me work
in a positive way
shine
sunshine
shine
your light
today

He took up
the wishbone.
"Wish for something,"
he said.
So I wished . . .
and then wished
that wishes could come true.
He smiled at me.
"What did you wish?"
And I looked at him,
warily
loving him.
"What did you wish?"
And he saw
my face and said,
"I wished what you wished."
And I smiled
and I wished
I could believe him.

You sweep my speak,
with the coarse yard broom,
carelessly on the front doorstep
where my words become confused
with the letters on the dirty *WELCOME* mat.

Were they not worthy
of a spot,
the bottom shelf, even,
of the curio cabinet?
I never asked for them
juxtaposed with
the Fabergé eggs.

And so as ignorant drops of rain
dissolve my vowels
and make slimy slivers
of my punctuation marks,
I curse you,
you could have honored me, at least,
with the dignity of the garbage bin.

Calabash Writer's Workshop Fellow

Cloaked reports of shotguns . . .
all the fathers are out,

birds flying over.
I'm tugging at the trigger

of the little shotgun
Rosalind never used,

but it doesn't move.
Baldpate and whitewing

are flying past.
"Yuh got de savety on,"

Jabez says, and shows me.
I'm too tired to walk,

so Jabez carries me
all the way back.

I don't say thank you
to Jabez. He's my friend.

No, I have not
Lost my marbles
I am throwing them
Far away
One by one

I do not
Want to play anymore
Unless we change

the Rules.

Calabash Writer's Workshop Fellow

Walking backward from the sea,
scales shedding, you seek the cave.

This is why the French door admits
only ocean. You stare into the louver

and forget how to get out. Lull
is the word, or loll. The sea returns,

completing your pulse, the waves live,
each breath of yours worship.

For my father

Overhead, pelicans glide in threes —
    their shadows across the sand
        dark thoughts crossing the mind.

Beyond the fringe of coast, shrimpers
    hoist their nets, weighing the harvest
        against the day's losses. Light waning,

concentration is a lone gull
    circling what's thrown back. Debris
        weights the trawl like stones.

All day, this dredging — beneath the tug
    of waves — rhythm of what goes out,
        comes back, comes back, comes back.

PART II: MEDIUM

ABALONE

Chris Abani

1.

It is a tenderness, this way
waves rough the shore —
like love, like a moon so full
the ocean cannot sleep for want of it.
And a woman beholds the voice of her lover
in this murmur: water over rock, over sand.

2.

On a beach in Nigeria, vines heavy with gourds
sound the loss of kin to a pugnacious sea.
On a beach in Jamaica, the other side of Africa's heart,
gourds grow vascular and full, and a reluctant people
carve a presence from it, a light in swirls
like the guitar's stutter that calls for home
in every chekem of the lick and step and block and slide — chaa!
And a stage like the carved-out shell of a calabash holds the song.

3.

My people say: the riddle of our being is in the calabash.
My people say: as big as the sea is, a calabash can hold it.
My people say: there is no loss a bottle gourd cannot contain.
My people say: love is an unending hymn —
a tie left in the grass by a child's hands,
a knot against tomorrow and the fickle wind.

Mbubu is the name of an Afikpo mask carved from a calabash gourd.

FEMINIST POEM NUMBER ONE

※

Elizabeth Alexander

Yes I have dreams where I am rescued by men:
my father, brother, husband, no one else.
Last night I dreamed my brother and husband
morphed into each other and rescued me
from a rat-infested apartment. "Run!"
he said, feral scampering at our heels.
And then we went to lunch at the Four Seasons.

What does it mean to be a princess?
"I am what is known as an American Negro,"
my grandmother would say, when "international friends"
would ask her what she was. She'd roller-skate
to Embassy Row and sit on the steps of the embassies
to be certain the rest of the world was there.

What does it mean to be a princess?
My husband drives me at 6 a.m.
to the airport an hour away, drives home,
drives back when I have forgotten my passport.
What does it mean to be a princess? I cook
savory, fragrant meals for my husband
and serve him, if he likes, in front of the TV.
He cooks for me, too. I have a husband.

In the dream we run into Aunt Lucy,
who is waiting for a plane from "Abyssinia"
to bring her lover home. I am the one
married to an Abyssinian, who is already here. I am the one
with the grandmother who wanted to know the world.
I am what is known as an American Negro princess,
married to an African prince,
living in a rat-free apartment in New Haven,
all of it, all of it, under one roof.

1.
My mother cooked with salt,
flavoring our lives
with the spice of her choice . . .
A white grain from the sea
that added new worlds of taste
to children made of mixed spices.

2.
My father loved his pepper
heating up her pot
with its red flames,
that little masculine bulb
men use to show brav-
ado about nothing.

3.
We ate of Mother's salt
all of our lives till we grew
old enough to insist
she travel to the sea
of her spice, a-
way from the red heat
of our father's pepper.

4.
Today, fifteen years on
my mother has stopped
cooking with that spice
as white as my father's skin.
And we have grown accus-
tomed to his hot spice,

hardly remembering
her love for little white grains
drawn from the sea.

Calabash Writer's Workshop Fellow

THOSE WHO DUG LESTER YOUNG ARE NOT SURPRISED . . .   *Amiri Baraka*

Those who dug Lester Young are not surprised
        But those
Who can't understand
What they did, can't understand
Who they are. Are then lost, in the moss, lost to the discourse
Uncorrected, misdirected, uninspected, unprotected,
never seen or known them or they, we and us, all, y'all
so then be unknown to most except the host
who told them they ain't who they is
so insist they is who they ain't, it's quaint, just add
a little paint, and say the same brain as the insane
and not know, who you, who he, who we, blind like in Spanish
cannot si si see. As if race was a waste it is, horse number three ain't none of we.
And class was it true, others the same as you, but on your head, if you
upside down, they underground, that's cool, it's romantic
you get frantic, they answer's antic, like the guy
who crawl up out the bottle and want to know if you got his bubble.
But pleas to make you understand, you is another breathing space
who got they own time and place. Come this far in a minute.
Ain't even outta breath, come this far so soon, don't know yrself.
Drunk some coon swoon, 145 years that's a beginndin again
44=08, start in 09 equals the time, and it's 10, one again. Come so far so quick.
They forget to tell you wasn't just slow you wasn't just uneducated
you was slick, you wasn't just all heart, you was also very smart.
How you think you was drug over here in chains, next thing we know
you the president! Goddamn, you think you could survive amongst this hostile tribe
and not be smart, plus tough, w/all that heart. Those who dug Lester Young
would understand . . . Wha's happenin, Prez?

Gwan trod

Even though nutten nah gwan

Gwan trod

Even though you going through a storm

Gwan trod

Even though the hill look high

The most high the almighty one

A guide you and I

Youth you know

You know fi hold a vibes

Youth men get wise

Try fi realize

Jah inna you and I

You nah go see him

Inna de sky

Baby mother get up

And gwan try

Look inna yuself

Seek the most high

The one who create the earth

The fish the sea and everything inna di sky

Fights, plights, am I never right?

In some badmind people

And some hypocrite sight

But me know who a guide

Over I day and night

And me know who & who

holding dung poetry fi spite

And me know myself

And I do things different

In this world mi be miself

Isn't that apparent

Gwan trod

You will own your own apartment

Gwan trod

One day you will stop pay rent

Gwan trod

Even though nutten nah gwan

Gwan trod

Even though you going through a storm

Gwan trod

Calabash Writer's Workshop Fellow

Derek Bennett, killed by the police

after Matisse's *Icare (Jazz)*, 1947

I who born
Thirty-one years
Since the *Windrush* come
Thirty-one years
Life of a man
I who born
Six gold bullets
Life of a man
I who born

    & because we suck the neon of the streets
    & because we tote a solar plexus of islands (*it's true*)
    & because we yuck out the blue heart of night (*right*)
    & because our heads gather thick as a bloodclot (*teach them*)
    & because we eat out the honey of mad laughter (*every time*)
    & because we outrun the delirium of streetlights (*more fire*)
    & because we are bugs scuttling from the lifted rock
    & because & because & &
    & because my eyehole grows iridescent with the moon
    & because we holler for the bloodclad sun
    & because we mourn the burst testes of the stars
    & because we skank cross rivers of blood

Mine New Cross mine Oldham Notting Hill Bradford Brixton mine
too Nassau Laventille Bridgetown Kingston Britain has branded an
x this rolled throat of killings this septic eye of maggotry this seed of
Mars this blasted plot this hurt realm this ogly island this England

---

They were not wrong—blonde mother, blonde daughter—
To laugh: Their dark driver dazzled; he jested
Wantonly, was jauntily seductive.
Courteous, cordial, proper, politic,
He lavished wit impeccably impish,
Encyclopedia-posh, and polished—
With scholarly asides and rhymester's timing,
Prompting the ladies' yielding gaiety,
To be repaid, he could hope, handsomely,
With a pretty tip (that common homage).
   So when their courtly, coppery chauffeur
Claimed to have a poet-son, it seemed cute.
But his passengers were polite enough
To commute their blithe doubt to nods and smiles,
To giggle privately, at homecoming,
At the audacity of their driver,
To expect them to credit him—a hack
Operator, despite his suave grammar
And stunning puns—with fathering a son
Who could credibly be declared poet.
   He never knew their laughing disbelief,
Which was fair, casual, and jocular fun:
As far as they knew, men whose livelihoods
Are step-and-fetch-it stereotypes—black chaps
Delivering white ladies and luggage
Delicately to the appointed address—
Are not expected to sire any bard.
   I heard their apology for this apt
Assumption, almost tearful, but tactful,
As I taxi'd a book into their hands,
And spoke almost as graciously, graceful,
As my unparalleled father would have.

That time my grandmother dragged me
through the perfume aisles at Saks, she held me up
by my arm, hissing, "Stand up,"
through clenched teeth, her eyes
bright as a dog's
cornered in the light.
She said it over and over,
as if she were Jesus,
and I were dead. She had been
solid as a tree,
a fur around her neck, a
light-skinned matron whose car was parked, who walked
       on swirling
marble and passed through
brass openings—in 1945.
There was not even a black
elevator operator in Saks.
The saleswoman had brought velvet
leggings to lace me in, and cooed,
as if in the service of all grandmothers.
My grandmother had smiled, but not
hungrily, not like my mother
who hated them, but wanted to please,
and they had smiled back as if
they were wearing wooden collars.
When my legs gave out, my grandmother
dragged me up and held me like God
holds saints by the
roots of the hair. I begged her
to believe I couldn't help it. Stumbling,
her face white
with sweat, she pushed me through the crowd, rushing

away from their eyes
that saw through
her clothes, under
her skin, all the way down
to the transparent
genes confessing.

A young moose bleeds behind a perforated truth.
Two targets, one bullet.
The older hunter quickly takes cover.
Dangerous business this blind shooting.
The ice queen paints a bisected country, a fair appraisal.
Indeed bitter heritage still jellied and jarred by old white hands
beneath obdurate flags
in belts where Jesus still wouldn't want you to bring home a negro.
Yet one where miscegenated marches dared the hoses of a "bull"
and now enough, just enough for change.
Politicians are idealistic lianas chasing their refulgent egos.
Too poetic the patient sword
but people need messiahs.
Now he, the unwilling chameleon,
infectious, a tall glass of easy
smiles calmly before cannibals
playing buttered words with lanky Miles-like restraint
thoughts deftly machined into audible fine print
he juggles close to the floor
the magnificent tenacity of desert grass
now the .44 resolver
he carves him a spot in the domino
deep enough for a people.
The audacity!
Those mulattoes never did know their place.
Uncivil war's rare victory.
The children with miner's eyes still sniff the air
for hunters lurk.
Old man river smiles, finally breaks silence,
his first words,
the one drop rule-s.

I will ignore you (tormentors). I will not let you know
that I know you are right there.
—Pumpsie Green, Boston Red Sox (1959–1962)

If the ball be white, then praise to Pumpsie,
who carried Anansi the Spider God to late 1950s Boston,

first black player for the Red Sox, last team in
America to let black players on the field.

Sometimes, they say, Anansi appears as a spider,
sometimes he's just some guy who looks like a guy,

but then funny things happen. He can slope his
fingers around things forbidden, hot sun, white moon,

toss it up where it hadn't belonged.
Why is that moon in the sky? we ask.

That's the joy beneath impossible tossing.
For the young black man in a field of white faces,

how did it feel to walk through a hive
of bees? Who sent the lifting winds?

Did a black man really steal fire
right under the nose of the Gods?

light me
she whispered

fire free
and sweet
water rages
reigns outside

taste me
she tempted

blended beat
itching for heat
wrapped
rolled
ready for a ride

check me
she urged

flip the cover
pluck
probe
pick a stick
find the edge

slide the red
bulbous head
on velvet sulphur
singe air
sing smoke
shape clouds

blue gray follows
flaming head
shifting swirling
like trance
after-rhythm
hisses implosion
in the belly
of his dance
and
my spent stick
crumbles too soon

but rest
breathe

and here
I come again

Calabash Writer's Workshop Fellow

With you I'm over easy
sliding down
spreading sunshine
for sticks of toast
golden then gooey
on a protracted Sunday morning.
You are chef and connoisseur
preparing and consuming
because you can
because I let you
because I want you to.
See, I was scrambled before
adulterated by other than
what I am,
confused by complex recipes
for what-should-be
on rye
drawn to exotic and faraway flavors
that don't quite fit
with eggs.
But you
break me open
see me as I am
and love me with
a little heat
so that I can simply be myself
over easy
and with you.

THE SWIMMING POOL AT VILLA GRIMALDI

Martín Espada

Santiago, Chile

Beyond the gate where the convoys spilled their cargo
of blindfolded prisoners, and the cells too narrow to lie down,
and the rooms where electricity convulsed the body
strapped across the grill until the bones would break,
and the parking lot where interrogators rolled pickup trucks
over the legs of subversives who would not talk,
and the tower where the condemned listened through the wall
for the song of another inmate on the morning of execution,
there is a swimming pool at Villa Grimaldi.

Here the guards and officers would gather families
for barbeques. The interrogator coached his son:
Kick your feet. Turn your head to breathe.
The torturer's hands braced the belly of his daughter,
learning to float, flailing at her lesson.

Here the splash of children, eyes red
from too much chlorine, would rise to reach
the inmates in the tower. The secret police
paraded women from the cells at poolside,
saying to them: *Dance for me.* Here the host
served chocolate cookies and Coke on ice
to the prisoner who let the names of comrades
bleed down his chin, and the lungs of the prisoner
who refused to speak a word ballooned
with water, facedown at the end of a rope.

When a dissident pulled by the hair from a vat
of urine and feces cried out for God, and the cry
pelted the leaves, the swimmers plunged below the surface,
touching the bottom of a soundless blue world.

From the ladder at the edge of the pool they could watch
the prisoners marching blindfolded across the landscape,
one hand on the shoulder of the next, on their way
to the afternoon meal and back again. The neighbors
hung bedsheets on the windows to keep the ghosts away.

There is a swimming pool at the heart of Villa Grimaldi,
white steps, white tiles, where human beings
would dive and paddle till what was human in them
had dissolved forever, vanished like the prisoners
thrown from helicopters into the ocean by the secret police,
their bellies slit so the bodies could not float.

ZENOBIA, APAPA DOCKS
LAGOS, 1949

Bernardine Evaristo

She stood there in her best blue wrapper and head tie,
the silent Zenobia, and the sea poured out of her.

She stood there until the ship had pulled out of harbor,
out of sight. Still, she stood there, listening

to the waves against the harbor walls. She looked out
onto the Slave Coast, Bight of Benin, the Atlantic

which had brought Gregorio from Brazil, and Baba.
Forever she stood there, watched the clouds converge,

prayed that her boy Taiwo would be safe on his journey,
happy in his new home. She thought of her marriage

without love, her childhood home in Abeokuta, Kehinde
about to give birth, and Baba—who was watching her now.

And she did not feel the salt sea stream down her face,
did not feel the steady breeze blow in from parts

of the world she would never know; and when the stars
appeared in the deepening sky, she felt a tug at her arm,

it was Kehinde, come to lead her from that place
which gave life, took life, and she knew with a mother's love

that the sea would not bring her son back.

*An excerpt from the verse novel *Lara*.

i was a fine violin
till i broke in half
could not take the pressure
n split

now i sit
gluing myself with prayer
and gentle song

each day a little here a little here
calling on the master musician
to touch
where i can't reach

he places his hand in the small
of my spine

my seams fuse together
perhaps more beautiful than before
perhaps more fine

perhaps these cracks
others follow with their fingers like a map
ahhh, I know that place
see how she came together
here n here

i was complete once

now
completing
gluing myself with prayer
and gentle song

and in my ears the music
of the master

The past moving behind these words
turning like a man in sleep
in the midst of a recurring dream. The past
coming to life in this strange yet familiar spot
near the shining Gulf-of-Guinea water
by the Door of No Return.

The past moving these words. Nothing
to mask the perseverance of memory.
Not the repetition of drumbeat. Not rain
nor the change coming with daybreak.
This is the spot where my forefather kneeled
to the presence of his daughter's screaming.

A past leading these words to the weeping room
still in full sight of the courtyard chapel.
This is the spot. Nothing
to lighten the circumstance,
not the sun-smeared floor of stone. Not moon
nor the whitewashed castle wall.

The swells of a past lifting these words
like a paper boat on deep water; and I
under a still-silent sky
muse through the deepening silence
by this Door of No Return.
No one can lift a drink to this.

It is good to praise god in the body
of the grandmother who is dead. Holy love
of bread & lovers who held your hand
as they kissed the soft meat between your legs, yes,
Grandmother, I am singing to you
though the lyrics make you cover your face, I want you
to be kissed again, even if only in songs. Like that.
My head is full of ideas, so I say your name
as I am building the houses
of the city in this poem. I am walking
through the night's alleys,
alleys of stars & crickets saying
your name into the wall where the neighbors moan
in a dark room on the other side of my home.
Grandmother, animals running
through the gates of their lovers, then fields,
is old news. It does not pull you from the ground
or wake you from a sleep beneath
the cemetery's stones & cactus.
On my life, on mud & starlight,
I want to dress my voice in horses
& send them back 60 years, Haragu,
to stand silver nights outside your marriage window
singing Bless you, Grandmother, in Gondar.
You thought you were dreaming. The red horses you saw
when your husband touched your ankle with his mouth.
What is the sound of two lines crossing? *Haragu* —
What is the word a body makes
when it opens in the night or day?
Haragu, Haragu — The touched body breaks
into a flock of birds eventually. There
at first, then vanishing
like the stars.

I feel it coming on again, the glow
the tightening, lord god
I would stop it if I could

but the fingers keep playing me
the whispers keep saying it is time
my love, my love, let go

I am full and green and going
there again is not what I want
but I can never stop it when it goes this far

don't stop, don't stare at me please
the gold you see is lost control to me
and in this moment I belong to anyone who wants me

there, there, I am yours
my yellow madness in full view
you smile and think my blooming is god's gift to you

but any number can have me
in these days, until flowers fall
all spread below me
like a yellow skirt pulled down

and then my brown and naked limbs
get rest, until my time comes round again

Calabash Writer's Workshop Fellow

Your shadow climbs on top my half
of the divan; the damp patch of you
is cooled by an oscillating fan.

Underneath a fitted sheet forgets,
losing its crush to a day not yet solid
but a cut of gentian violet.

Sleep till I come;
I go with the worn-out moon
to Coronation to buy ground provision

from women with dirt-dried aprons
and earthstains under crescent nails
bundled in bales; women

like crushed leaves staining
the lining of hand-me-down linen
skirts; women bitter like medicine

calling out from yawning holes
the names of diggings,
their eyes on my bosom.

Leaning to one side, I tell time
by the lift of dust, the smell
of my pits; I know

that the dew on your forehead will soon drop
like ripe pears, purple and dangling.
Picking between death or dying

I whisper *Stay*
to the moon leaving me to carry the crocus,
and *Don't raise up* to the sun.

Sleep, sleep till I come,
don't raise up till I come.

ROOT *Sabrina Hayeem-Ladani*

For Dorianne Laux

I had to do it—
took your book of poems from my bag this morning, plucked
the sleek ocean jacket from the bulging depths of my purse
to lighten the load. Beat-up flamenco shoes, already
wanting to be worn, pushed through the thin fleece fiber.

Not enough room for the dance and poetry today.
Not for you or your men, making love
between the coffee table and couch, or standing up
against the dishwasher while the kids sleep.
These letters to your naked lover, homage to a tree,
were simply too heavy to be slung over my shoulders
from morning until night.

I'm sorry, Dorianne, but these are the facts about flamenco:
I am anchored to its bloodied heart, furious rhythm
of a gypsy woman's dance, outcry of the poor and forgotten
melting the mountains of Andalusia. It's the tragedy
that gets me—burst of the demon from its dusty cave,
wings flapping a funeral hymn. These dancers dare
to sleep inside fire. Resplendent, they till the earth
clad in flames, dig their heels into soil, and mourn.

This is why, packing my bag this morning,
I chose the dance over you—to pound my swollen feet
into the hard wooden floor, instead of cracking open
your book, running my fingers over the finely printed text.

But tonight . . . deal me in.
You, kind poet, skilled wordsmith of my heart and sex.
Read me facts about the moon. Show me

how you take the root of love and uncoil it,
fingertips sticky with bark and sap.
Teach me how we women tend to hold things,
then give them over to life:
to be the vestibule, the oven, the house.
You, glorious storyteller of everything I am trying to dance.

The mouth is where the dead
Who are not dead do not dream

A house of damaged translations
Task married to distraction

As in a bucket left in a storm
A choir singing in the rain like fish

Acquiring air under water
Prayer and sin the body

Performs to know it is alive
Lit from the inside by reckoning

As in a city
Which is no longer a city

The tongue reaching down a tunnel
And the teeth wet as windows

Set along a highway
Where the dead live in the noise

Of their shotgun houses
They drift from their wards

Like fish spreading thin as a song
Diminished by its own opening

Split by faith and soaked in it
The mouth is a flooded machine

love
why don't you come to me
gently
persistently
as calculated as the regulated ticking
of a clock
the love of a quiet man
a weekday man
a man that brings me roses
but not orchids
a kind man with friendly eyes
and regimental habits
but I have been seduced
by Friday night
neon lights
and muted jazz seeping up
from dingy doorways
car horns
and lovers quarreling
loud and unashamed
a streetbulb reflected in a puddle
garbage cans
and yesterday's newspapers
and love
given widely
chance meetings
and flirtations of the night
asking nothing more
than that Friday night may end
as Friday night began
taking with her
all she gave
and leaving nothing
for tomorrow

SUMMER RICE *Linda Susan Jackson*

After Nikky Finney

They're up to their necks in fever and floodplains, clear-
ing ground along miles of riverbed, bloodred. Carolina heat
burns holes in their straw hats, leaves halos of steam around
silhouettes. Down the line, they are one deep breath riding
field rhythms *Movin', movin'.* Lone bones of things: a dog's jaw,
a man's leg, a baby's pelvis; thin bones of turtles, birds, fish
pulled to the surface by swole-up hands. Hopsack dresses
singe the women's bodies. Fringes hang from straw pants on
sweat-soaked, bare-chested men in the line. The line shouter
urges them on *Movin' on down the line. Huh.* The searing sun
drives quail points in their backs, its red glare shedding circles
of light around their darkening bodies. Foot after foot of earth
unearthed. Root-thick soil dug up along low country rivers
for glaberrima, Africa's rice. Heels indent soil for seeds; big
toes cover seeds with soil in song *You told me, huh, knees are
important.* Gnarled fingers of grans and nans who no longer
winnow, weave ancient designs into coiled baskets of pine,
sweet grass, bulrush and palmetto to hold the summer yield.
Hulls beat against hollowed-out trees as they whirl in dervish
frenzy, carried round by ringing words *Movin' on down the line,
huh.* Despite bits and whips, they return to thatched-roof huts,
sweep up dusty dirt with palm-leaf brooms before they bank
the dinner fire. Lean-to chimneys ride smoke and ash up mud
walls, a calico headscarf on a nail, the room's only rush of
color. Their bodies break down on straw pallets. Tomorrow,
same as today. Same as yesterday. Okra and tomato stew.
Fish on Sunday, scratching out the scream holler of summer
rice in their bones *Ah'm a movin'. Movin' out the line. Huh.*

Try to catch the deluge in a paper cup . . .
There's a hole in the roof
—Crowded House

What's in a cup?
Ice, mountains
smell of coffee
that's what, she told me
leaning by the kitchen door
feet unsteady, her chin in the air
and that puckered frown, as much to capture
questions as release them from limbo.

Speckled with flour, the recipe
overturned by a breeze, we labored
piles of words like thickets of rosemary
plunging our hands in the metal bowl
until the dough was too spent
to do anything but sigh, listless
at our child's game.

So much rain.
To make the flowers grow
she said, drawing circles on the counter
adding lightning stems
for the measure.

The dough sat in the fridge now
bloated, waiting to be pounded again.
I wiped the counter, relieving the flowers
of their frenzied growing. Mere zeros
the circles, like pockets of moondust
drizzling by the window.

Calabash Writer's Workshop Fellow

We took a boat down the Black River,
The water darker than the darkest mirror,
The mangrove roots trailing the riverbed—
As if searching for the dead down there.
We passed a tree shocked by the hurricane
Whose spindly limbs had transformed
Into a Rastafarian's dreadlocks
Rising from the riverbed's rocks.
We passed crocodiles masquerading as logs
Under the mangroves, and snow egrets
Fluttering like blossoms in the branches,
And the river carried us as if carrying us home—
Wherever we were, wherever we came from:
A black river running through our arteries,
A black river putting our hearts at ease,
A black river touching our skin like a lover,
A black river to remind us of our ancestors,
Running through the swamps and secret marshes
When freedom was a belief the river rushes
Passed along the dark water like a breeze.
Then, later, when the river ran to meet the sea,
And the colors changed—black, to brown-black, to bright blue—
There was my son at the helm of the boat
As the boat lifted and crashed and smashed on the waves,
And there were the jackfish leaping,
The dolphins' diasporic dive, and those strange birds
—whose name I have forgotten—
Carrying an old song home.

MAMBA MUNTU READS POETRY IN THE CARIBBEAN

Ann-Margaret Lim

For Sonia Sanchez

The sea greets me, but I feel too the pain
let me turn my back, instead of a face
to the sea of the Caribbean.

And the sea echoed
and swelled
as she read at the festival.

It pounded.
And exploded.
And as she leaked beads of sea

a poem trembled in my skin
to know: the black pearl eyes
deep, and calm, and agitated as the sea

drowned with this woman
who swallowed the sea.
And when it was time

she suctioned herself whole —
black pearl eyes,
seaweed locks, moody, like the sea

and a balm of deep-sea poetry
for the kinsmen, scattered like
shells on the beaches of the Caribbean.

Calabash Writer's Workshop Fellow

Blood pride
gorged with the taint
of flight and massacre, heaved.
Ojukwu
arose each day
with the nation's hopes
and at evening strode
through a million dreams.
Black love grew
in white cities
in far world corners
in eyes
filled with wonder
sadder
than the anguish
in those
huge numb eyes
of a broken nation's
bloated children.
Black hearts hardened
against pity, tears
or black blood
pursued
a sullen victory.

Now mark Uli
where the spirit's sad flight
lies broken;
how memory closes
on the place
where the dream was
erasing the dream.

Calabash Writer's Workshop Fellow

You gave me a white flower
with its eyes closed,
pages of white paper
without print.
It reminded me
of a Chinese ambassador.
I am afraid of this flower
for walls are white;
they say light is white
and that white is often wrong.
My flower will open
only at night.

Night is a neighbor's room;
I can just see the door
as it closes.
We are saints without worlds
and we wait for the sun.
My flower
stretched herself tight
like an opaque gloom;
she has no face
only one blind eye
that doesn't glow.
Night is a crematorium
at work in the next room,
angels of white wax,
flowers with white canes.

Lorne Matthews

Month of February

I am a seed shaped sweetly,
kicks in my mother's belly.
I cannot see her red skin,
her coarse hair aflame,
her moist hands soothing
the growth that is her son.
She is ready for April.
I grow restless for April.
Her things are placed neatly
in a bag beside the bed.

Month of March

There is a quarrel; words jostling,
the footsteps of my father, falling
heavy, then silent. I cannot see
the tears of my mother, drip, trickling to her breasts,
the wet curved along the flesh
bustling restless with life.

My father is busy betting my pampers and crib;
he is a fourth head at cards, turned dizzy with rum.
I imagine him a shallow man, none too eloquent for the liquor:
he has forfeited his duty to secure my gripe water.
I cannot see his grin, one soon I will carry. I cannot see his eyes
set searching for clues. I cannot see the hand he'll lose
or tell him of April, tell him of a Tuesday, how soon I'd come.

Month of April

My mother is straining; her belly aimed forward, her red back sweating
is turned to my father. I cannot see her feet, swollen, how they draw
over concrete. Or her lips wet, muttering the words of a resolve.

I am a seed expelled, shot brown into whiteness, into air (first breaths of it),
a crying speech for a tongue.
I can see my mother, her white teeth smiling;
I can see my father, his black back leaving.

Calabash Writer's Workshop Fellow

a woman moves through dog rose and juniper bushes,
a pussy clean and folded between her legs,
breasts like the tips of her festive shoes
shine silently in her heavy armoire.

one black bird, one cow, one horse.
the sea beats against the wall of the waterless.
she walks to a phone booth that waits
a fair distance from all three villages.

it's a game she could have heard on the radio:
a question, a number, an answer, a prize.
her pussy reaches up and turns on the light in her womb.

from the rain, she says into the receiver,
we compiled white tables and chairs under a shed
into a crossword puzzle
and sat ourselves in the grid.

the receiver is silent. the bird flounces
like a burglar caught red-handed.
her voice stumbles over her glands.
the body to be written in the last block —
i can suck his name out of any letter.

all three villages cover their faces with wind.

She brought the radish for the horses, but not a bouquet for
Mother's Day. She brought the salad to order with an unleav-
ened joke. Let us dive in and turn up green in search of our
roots. She sang the union maid with a lefty longshoreman.
They all sang rusty freedom songs, once so many tongues
were loosened. She went to bed sober as always, without a
drop of wine. She was invited to judge a spectacle. They were
a prickly pair in a restaurant of two-way mirrors with rooms
for interrogation. The waiter who brought a flaming dessert
turned the heat from bickering to banter. She braked for jerk
chicken on her way to meet the patron saint of liposuction.
His face was cut from the sunflower scene, as he was stuffing
it with cheesecake. Meanwhile, she slurped her soup alone
at the counter before the gig. Browsers can picture his un-
censored bagel rolling around in cyberspace. His half-baked
metaphor with her scrambled ego. They make examples of
intellectuals who don't appreciate property. She can't just
trash the family-style menu or order by icon. Now she's mak-
ing kimchee for the museum that preserved her history in a
jar of pickled pig feet. They'd fix her oral tradition or she'd
trade her oral fixation. Geechees are rice eaters. It's good to
get a rice cooker if you cook a lot of rice. Please steam these
shellfish at your own risk. Your mother eats blue-green algae
to rid the body of free radicals.

Yu have dis whole heap a words a suppressed inside a yu.
It might fly up in yu head and mad yu too.
As di lyrics dem come, write dem dung.
When pain rack yu soul and illusions tek ova yu dream,
give yu thoughts permission to scream.
Most tings in life come wid a price.
Words come to me free.
When norms, rules, and regulations
a pull mi inna all different direction, dem act as cushions.
Form fence, bar out intruders,
tek di blows so mi don't have broke bones.
Even if di world a fall apart, a feel safe inside mi heart.
Jus a cut and go through, sharp-edge rhymes
laced wid political meaning, claiming but not explaining.
No style, no rhythm, no discipline, no imagery, no magic.
Raw, free spirit, come to challenge yu frozen rhetoric.
Conservatives fi know, dem fi low it, mek it grow,
it done a show.
Your circumsized vision cannot damage dis one.
Charge mi fi lyrical treason,
mi still a go exercise mi poetic license.
Desire's on fire,
right ya now wi need two more poems fi inspire.
So tek da lazy-ass poem deh off a di paper.
Mek mi chant it like a mantra:
work to be done, send di poem come.
Dis a no Anglo-Saxon English.
Some a dem words ya,
yu naa go find inna Oxford or Webster.
Words decorated inna mi native tongue
a come from deep dung a bellie bottom.
Send di poem come, work to be done,

send di poem come.
A weh it do, mek unu lock it up inna book.
Dust and cobweb a feed dem lust.
Meanwhile poems a cohabitate.
Di poet a masterbate.
Send di poem come, work to be done,
send di poem come.

WILD NIGHT *Marilyn Nelson*

N.Y. Antiabolition Riots, 1834–1835
Rev. Christopher Rush

The white folks were restless again last night.
All we could do was keep the faith, and wait.
My first parishioners started arriving at sunset,
having heard rumors, and reluctant to stay at home.
Our shadows danced in the sanctuary's candle flames
as audible whiffs of pandemonium
drifted to us like smoke from distant fires.
With most of the village in, I locked the doors.

I asked everyone to bow their heads and pray.
Pray for this nation's struggle to be free
for ALL Americans. Equality
must be bitter, if you've always been on top,
and you're slapped awake out of a lifelong sleep.
Pray we'll pull together toward a common hope.

. . . Thousands of voices raised . . . That sounds like drums!
That sounds like a firehouse bell . . . That sounds like screams!

Near dawn. The children and some mothers sleep;
roosters crow morning, a couple of yard dogs yap,
the songbirds choir. The violence has stopped.
I step out into everyday new light.
My little flock has weathered a wild night.
But someone somewhere is less fortunate.
Tim Seaman comes out, nods, and finds a tree.
Would every now held such tranquility.

The other day my grown and married daughter
said to me, "I sound like this because I have the flu.
Daddy's on his way over here. But he might be

at the supermarket now. I guess he's buying Milo."
"Milo?" I asked? "Yes," she said chuckling,
"he buys me Milo whenever I'm sick.

In fact, it doesn't matter what I'm sick with.
Awhile ago the weather changed,
I got bronchitis and he bought me Milo.

He bought me Milo when they lost my papers
and I had to have that vaccine all over again.
And the day they came and towed away Plym

and I cried (her first car had finally died)
or when I've just had a bad day.
In fact, I've got tins of it in my cupboard."

And I think to myself,
I might have saved a good deal
of my marriage to this guy, had I known.
Back then I'd given him love,
much talk and copious tears, when Milo,
cups and cups of it, might have done the job!

*Sweetheart, should you run out of room
in your cupboard,
keep the space in your heart open;
that's what he's after.*

It began with the usual insults
about her nose and hips,
and the belief that her true-true mother
lived on a coral island protected
by sunken galleys and man-o'-wars.

These fantasies,
her therapists said, were drawing her
toward a different future
than her parents had wished for
when they punished her
for not reading the books they'd studied,
and sent her away on Easter egg hunts
dressed in starched, pink dresses, white bonnets,
and blue bows in each braid of her stubborn hair.

And when she began cutting her wrists,
arms, legs, and belly, her parents
agreed with the psychiatrists
to the prescriptions of pills, potions,
and poisons to keep her grounded in this life.

But then, the scabs became scars became scales,
her hair grew wild and untamed,
and a garden of yellows, blues, and reds sprouted
on her arms, legs, and back —
her ears and lips studded with gold —
and almost overnight she changed into something
she had always resembled in her own dreams,
in the mirror of her mother —
something beautiful and fearsome.

When I had no roof I made
Audacity my roof. When I had
No supper my eyes dined.

When I had no eyes I listened.
When I had no ears I thought.
When I had no thought I waited.

When I had no father I made
Care my father. When I had
No mother I embraced order.

When I had no friend I made
Quiet my friend. When I had no
Enemy I opposed my body.

When I had no temple I made
My voice my temple. I have
No priest, my tongue is my choir.

When I have no means fortune
Is my means. When I have
Nothing, death will be my fortune.

Need is my tactic, detachment
Is my strategy. When I had
No lover I courted my sleep.

your lying dogs . . .
I step over and up, but down
into your room and dark display
your genius brain is scattered out
in solid chunks of purged debris
and I can read your mind—a book
on art, a fossil shell, some wires, ropes
for climbing, or caving, and swimming gear
beside a large part-burned candle
the bamboo table leg is stabbed
by one of your special knives
your father's photo stands behind
some bottles for natural cures
and you sit to read me poems

you're lying down
a freckled heap finally sleeping
your busy worry resting too
and I cannot put back your room
in order to recapture exploded shards
of dagger-shaped grief—my tears
are not salve enough to heal your head
you've lost yourself in forced dreams
of cool indifference, of billowing
snowdrifts, here where the sun
always shines

your lying face tells me stories
your confusion has kaleidoscopic beauty
and your looks are wearing down
you are losing, and so are we
the empty rum bottles and full ashtrays

echo the wasting of a life
and the triumph of ugly
that slaps my head away

your prayer beads are lying
in a bowl
that begs for alms

Calabash Writer's Workshop Fellow

You Can't Survive on Salt Water

Kalamu ya Salaam

—seven haiku for old orleans—

1.
dead dogs hang from trees
bloated barges sit on the
wrong side of levees

2.
dumb pigeons have flown
now it's people's turn to perch
roasting atop roofs

3.
a caravan of
yellow buses drowns because
the mayor can't drive

4.
official death counts
exclude so-called looters shot
on sight of their skin

5.
dry folk uptown hold
their noses, rejecting wet
people's funky stank

6.
things that go bump in
the night: your boat against a
dead baby's body

7.

a son returns, finds
four-month-old bones wearing his
missing mother's dress

For Max Roach

1
Nothing ends
every blade of grass
remembering your sound

2
your sounds exploding
in the universe return
to earth in prayer

3
as you drummed
your hands kept
reaching for God

4
the morning sky
so lovely imitates
your laughter

5
you came warrior
clear your music
kissing our spines

6
feet tapping
singing, impeach
our blood

7

you came drumming
sweet life on
sails of flesh

8

your fast beat
riding the air settles
in our bones

9

your drums
soloing our breaths into
the beat . . . unbeat

10
your hands
shimmering on the
legs of rain*

On the tombstone of Max Roach

DEAD STRAIGHT   ❧   *Olive Senior*

I'm traveling back home to you but it's an omen:
my road map's creased and torn along dead straight lines.

The hill and gully ride is over now and I'm flat out
on the dead straight highway with a toll.

Not a glimmer of the coastline as I try to make it home
to you through a forest of hotels as thick as thieves.

For the sea, the coves and beaches once seen through
seaside shacks and palm trees have been sold.

And the rest of us are herded to the verge by this new
highway while over there our beauty is extolled,

bottled and sold. And gated. In this new paradise the only
palms are greased. And somebody's beach umbrella

has replaced the shade tree we once sat under and the
towns and settlements molder as they are bypassed.

I can no longer witness on this highway with a toll that
makes us seem as modern as elsewhere. For elsewhere

is not where I'm meant to be. And a dead straight
highway leaves no scent, no monument to the past,

no scenic beauty for the curvature of my eye to take in.
And endless empty space is not inviting. But perhaps

there's no social meaning to this tirade after all. I'm just
feeling lost without a map as I make it home to you

and pay the toll. You could see it simply as a love song.
To the curving of your cheekbones, to the mountains

of your thighs, the hill and gully passion of your eyes, and
your hair that is not dead straight but very much otherwise.

TO THE MAN WHO TENDS MY GRANDMOTHER'S GRAVE

Tanya Shirley

I give you thanks for knowing the ways of the living,
how it is important for my mother to know her mother
has not been forgotten: last week a son brought three
faux flowers, wept like a child over her grave; the week
before Mrs. B, on her way to visit her daughter cut down
by sugar, stopped for a brief chat, laughing like old times.
I give you thanks for the plot of grass, perpetually green
in a place famous for water lock-offs and parched earth.
I give you thanks for stooping to Brillo polish her silver
tombstone so we see ourselves in the sheen.
I give you thanks for carrying the red dirt from all these
graves into your house each night, showing your children
that we are all half spirit, composites of the living and the dead.
I give you thanks for taking the crumpled bills, small
payment for back-breaking work in the sun, with a smile;
even when this exchange is infrequent like the rain here.
I give you thanks for knowing the slight bend of a body
carrying grief, the quiet before flood. Last Sunday we came
with my father to visit his brother freshly laid in the earth,
another grave for you to tend; we thought he was handling
it well, he could drive us home. Quickly you ushered me over,
"Him can't drive. Him soon bruk down bad, bad." My mother
drove, my father became the water within him.
And you who tend these graves, may your death find you
amongst familiar faces, grateful recipients of your tending.

Adziko Simba

and the chip-chip chop of jelly and cane
the cart man out again and
the windscreens showered with bottles and boxes and mint and
nuts and crackers and crix
and the begging tricks of the shuffling rags
the criminal act of the open palm
the tight-fisted hand behind the glass
slid safely shut and sealed away
from hungry gnawing at the bone
as buses gorge on schoolers crisply ironed, lightly greased and
pressed between the seats
'ductors defying gods of sense swing from doors half hinged and
rattle and bob to the boombox spewing gravely grain
the rockstone voice
vomiting vice,
innocents enticed to
sing along
while elders wilt in far back rows
humming hellfire
these church organs
gripping bosoms and bibles and Jesus and
visioning flocks
washed white as snow to stem the flow
of red down gullies and gutters slashing streets like scars
where taxi cars
weave on speed
heart attacks on wheels
blasting drivers
driven to exceed

driven to exceed
all limits
unconstrained
life as passa passa
all untamed
all peeled open
all revealed
the ever static change
the buzz. the heat. the same.
halfway hell and halfway heaven
pull up and come again.

ASKING FOR A HEART ATTACK

Patricia Smith

For Aretha Franklin

Aretha. Deep butter dipped, scorched pot liquor,
swift lick off the sugarcane. Vaselined knees
clack gospel, hinder the waddling south. 'retha.
Greased, she glows in limelit circle, defending
her presence with sanctified moan, ass rumbling
toward curfew's backstreets, where jukes still gulp silver.

Goddess of Hoppin John and bumped buttermilk,
girl know Jesus by His first name. She the one
sang His drooping down from ragged wooden T,
dressed Him in blood red shine, conked that holy head,
rustled up excuses for bus fare and took
the Deity downtown. They found a neon
backslap, coaxed the DJ and slid electric
till the lights slammed on. Don't know where you goin',
 who you goin' with, but you sho can't stay here.

Aretha taught the Almighty slow, dirty
words for His daddy's handiwork, laughed as He
first sniffed whiskey's surface, hissed Him away when
He sought to touch His hand to the blue in her.
She was young then, spindly and thin ribs paining,
her heartbox thrumming in a suspicious key.
So Jesus blessed her, opened her throat and taught
her to wail that way she do, Lawd she do wail
that way don't she do that wail the way she do
wail that way, don't she? That girl can wail that way.
Now when Aretha's fleeing screech jump from juke
and reach been-done-wrong bone, all the Lord can do
is stand at a wary distance and applaud.
Oh yeah, and maybe shield His heart a little.

So you question her several shoulders,
the soft stairs of flesh leading to her chins,
the steel bones of an impossible dress
gnawing raw into bubbling obliques?
Ain't your mama never schooled you in how
black women collect the world, build other
bodies onto our own? No earthly man
knows the solution to our hips, asses
urgent as sirens, our titties bursting
with traveled roads. Ask Aretha just what
Jesus whispered to her that night about
the gospel hidden in lard and sugar.
Then you'll know the reason black girls grow fat
away from the world, and toward each other.

Somebody said "Let's ban them . . .
Let's get some rope and hang them!"
And the angry mob gathered bearing guns and knives, pitchforks and axes
Then the government said "Wait! First let us collect their taxes!"
And in what they claim to be representation of their God above
Society imposed a law which made it illegal to love
And the angry mob herded them, branded them, tagged them
Chanted in unison "Burn out the fag them!"
And honestly, all I could see was people hurting people
People telling other people how they're supposed to be
And I know this puts me at odds with the mob but it looks pretty wrong to me!
Some of us don't even know why we hate them, to us it's all a game
Though most of us don't pray to God, we hurt others in his name
"It must be right cause Jesus said it" It scares me, and I pray that
We would stop quoting a man we never met and never heard him say that
The church reeks of hatred, from the pulpit to the pews through the rectory
to the steeple
Call it "weeding out the bad ones" I call it people hurting people
People making decisions designed to bring other people pain
Hurting, scarring, maiming, taking lives in Jesus' name
That someone chooses a different path, really, what's it to ya?
So much anger, hatred, lacing every hallelujah!
Now it's ok to kill, alright to steal, go ahead and rape, it's fine!
Extort! Do wrongs of every sort! We'll lead the world in crime!
Moral will bend over backward to accommodate us!
Cause after all, we're normal! Hurrah! Congratulate us!
We'll celebrate our "normalness" in everything we do
And woe be unto anyone who isn't "normal" too!
We'll do what it takes to make them see things through our eyes
If we must, decapitate those who refuse to compromise
There's no good destination when hatred is your vehicle
Call it what you will, it's still people hurting people

AT AN OLD CHURCH IN TRELAWNY

Andrew Stone

In commemoration of the total abolition of slavery, 1838

Outside, the ground is littered
with plastic bottles and styrofoam boxes.
A crosswind blows into my face
turning sweat cold against my skin.
My steps are bold, I think,
but my stomach tightens:
funerals are hard.
The congregants rise to sing
over the grief: a hundred voices
bounce off the cold stone walls.
Nothing new here.
Every stone is a monument
to the labor of slaves;
the floor is stained by old tears.
The printed programs tell us
Mass Kenneth lived and died,
the simple coffin at the front
is a brutally silent witness.
Afterward,
groups of mourners huddle
over food and conversation.
On one wall of the church, a plaque:

You were enthroned on a rock
The moon carved out its silver belly
Turned itself upside down
over your head

The Mediterranean approached on its knees
kissed the silver ring
on the middle toe
of your dangling left foot

Your gold-plated nail grazed my nipple
I was encouraged
You said I was incorrigible

But after all was said and done
much was said
little done

You led Mohammad to the mountain
But you didn't let him drink
I was thirsty
at the brink
of your fountain

Because my palms were not sweaty
you said I was not excited about you
I wanted to take my treasonous hands to the marketplace
have them both chopped off

We sucked sea salt from each other's lips
Hugged so close we became one
We're both crazy about each other

You said
But we also fear commitment
I swallowed again
Like drought drinks first rain

Still
after all was said and done
much was said
little done

Some women carry their lives
in a wobbly basket to the marketplace
where they sell cakes, pies, rice and beans
stew chicken, rum punch, Mauby and sweet plantains

some women make big pots of pig tails make
roast corn, cod fish and fried bakes
they make pig feet and black pudding
sell it around the Arima savanna
to send their children to school

some women do hair and wash people dirty clothes
to put a roof over their heads
to take care of an ailing mother
feed a pregnant daughter
provide for a missing husband

some women sew holes into their fingertips
burn their wrist frying hair
some women go to England to study nursing
go to America and work in white-lady kitchen
some women leave their children behind

and leave their children behind
with their dreams
and fill the hurt places with fat men
shiny cars and big big houses

some women buy and sell
build up, tear down and search and run
and never hear the wind
calling their names

SILENCE

Ralph Thompson

When the accustomed hum which I
Have long accepted as the absence
Of sound suddenly ceases,
The ensuing silence pours into my ears
Like syrup and I become profoundly deaf.

I have not heard, O Lord,
The lamentation of the poor,
Or the laughter of the rich.
Nor in my sojourn in foreign lands
Has the echo of a bud unfolding
To a rose disturbed my sleep.

The summer season washes across
My history like a sable brush
Loaded with water blurring the boundaries
Of exact events. I do not hear
Their consequences being watered down.

By December the sky cracks
And out of its fissures a cold wind
Swirls, stripping the leaves from their branches.
They drop like black tears into the gutters
Of cities but I am not awakened
By the splash of their weeping.

Age spots map their dominion
On the back of my hands and a voice
Whispers through the syrup,
"When you are old and your soul
Is shivering, the last stitch of its dream
Unraveling, pull this poem

Like a shawl around your shoulders.
Only the rags of words are left to warm
The marrow, once more the word made flesh."

The rain comes late, draws the afternoon into darkness,
no light where there should be light, no way to be but drenched
until it curves down over your lips. The taste of every living thing
is in the raindrop the way all things open their eyes inside
a single bloom in the garden that is now hushed in a robe.

Whatever you feel about it, whether you live for it or pray
for the rains to die, the water joins with all of us, tendon, bone,
artery, vein, saliva, everything that melts and goes hard, escapes
as air. The water brings a reunion for a moment with what we know
each time we breathe ourselves here or are forced to breathe.

If I write without color it is to obey the gray way rain brings
the past to us. The ten thousand are one giant palace with a room
for remembering, where you must stand alone, touch and believe
while it seems you are touching nothing and have gone all mad
in this life, this gift. We are sitting on a rock in the thick falling

of water, purple lilies are growing in the sun's ocean shadow,
sheep with golden wool are flying in the trees, a patient monkey
is bandaging a wounded blade of grass, the garden is a mesa,
seeds are mountain caves, the moon has gone infinite, made
two of its own selves for each of our palms. Now we have faces.

Miles out to sea on bamboo stilts
a house walks on water, proof of perfect faith.
Invisible sandbar abets the mirage,
foundation shuddering with each breaking wave.
Thatched with sea hay, salt-stiff like morning hair,
the roof is less cover than a rumor of shade.

Ashore, we build homes behind breakwalls, shade
our bets, trust cement or steel over stilts.
Braid back desire like unruly hair.
Rapunzel's ladder is fairy-tale faith
that breaks like a widow's mirage:
his boat returning home on the next wave.

I remember the red-hot days, waving
off doubt like island sun burning up shade,
the heavy past fading like a mirage.
Suspended on love's green stilts,
there was nothing improbable in our faith.
Gravity could not survive the nimbus of your hair.

Now the dream house is sinking. The sea's hairtrigger
temper, a raw and hungry wave
sweeps the floor out from under faith.
Water after a storm turns an unfamiliar shade,
won't support the miracle of stiltwalking,
pillars paling in mirage.

What lingers in the heart is no mirage,
like what grows on after death—fingernails, hair.
The body's house stoops and tilts,
resists the weight of the crushing wave.

I ask only this—when you pull down the last shade,
leave a sliver for the light—one hair crack of faith.

Sailors name daughters and ships Hope or Faith,
lace coffee with brandy to ward off the mirage
of lighthouses blinking falsely through fog and shade.
Bibles are just baskets for a lock of the beloved's hair,
kept beside the memory of the children's goodbye wave:
clambering atop shoulders, our bodies their stilts.

This love, a seahouse on stilts. This arrogance of faith.
The threatening wave is never just a mirage,
so we hang by a hair, cast doubt seaward, praying for shade.

PART III: LARGE

Photo © 2010 Sally Henzell

Sweet Lip

Roger Bonair-Agard

(a praise song for going home)

Praise the exorbitant crocuses
  the kiskadee whistles
 the light unnatural when the heart
  is breaking—when it is wrestling
to mend

Praise every sweat spent
  on the soft earth
 a gratitude every task completed
an amen

Praise the jack spaniard's nest crooked
  dangerous up under the eaves
  the broken spanish tiles
bleeding my soft hands

Praise the 24-hour lizard
  scampering from the woodpile
Praise its flight the reptiles
that come after it praise
their shed skins

Praise this gunshot ache in the rib
  the woman who still lives there
Praise the friends who have
no time for your grief
who come to the house on the eve
of your leaving
who bubble the pork pot on the ground
in your front yard who cover it
with the fig leaf from your mother's trees

Praise your mother's trees the bananas
  gone rotten and picked by birds
Praise the blackbird and morning dove

Praise the rum added last to the pot
  like a calling to spirits past
Praise your mother who carries
your pain like her own aching
hip

Praise her hip
  its new titanium joint
  the rain it predicts its bucket-a-drop
cascade the wonder of its volume
over which we shout to be heard

Praise us that we hear each other

When the light comes up, the kettle whistles. From your child-
hood bedroom you can see just how unnatural brilliant the blue
can be. Rub it into your heartbreak like a balm; that blue. Praise
the burn there, how beautiful this place—home where all your
histories have her face even if she has never seen this rising steam
from the pavement, this raucous corner bar, the yard you played
in, the flowers whose stems you sucked dry.

Praise the best friend who takes off
work to see you off at the airport
  his everlast love the way from the terminal
window the light is always bending
something new something far away

Even what is always there is changing
   now a garden, now the prison walls
   now the songs you sing in planting
   now the dirge you whistle in reaping

something always being given
something being taken
away

ISAIAH
de rastaman
tongue full of flames
red righteous brains
descend from de mountains
trod troo de plains
bringing a warning
to a nation gawn insane

ISAIAH
de nyaman
chanting fire troo de lan
talk like thunder touch im han
breathe brimstone pon Babylon
Israel, you forget God plan
no more burning dove or ram
no more sacrifice of lamb
no more fasting, no more prayer
God is deaf to your desire

ISAIAH
de rastaman
heart beating hard
no stone, no sword, no guard
talking every word de spirit declare
Israel, yuh forget yuh God
corruption mek yuh choose de bad
wickedness defile yuh
vain power start beguile yuh
de lust for blood done spoil yuh
if God neva mek dat promise to yuh
yuh woulda sink like Sodom an Gomorrah

yuh woulda run like yuh jus laas yuh shadow
today would be the end of yuh tomorrow
an yuh children would reap pure sorrow

ISAIAH
de iyaman
bow im head as im humbly stan
an big Israel come clean
to remember what love mean
an retreat from a murderous scene
stop pushing others to where you've been
you of all should find genocide obscene
God just might let yah een

ISAIAH
de binghiman
come to chant dung Babylon
day by day in burning sun
bringing de word of God anger
let Israel tremble and hear
why truth can fill de hunger
Israel be humble and prepare
God's wrath is drawing near
there's land enough to share
let covetousness disappear
offer up a humbler prayer

ISAIAH
de rastaman
let words burn across the lan
an wait for God to play im han

Now, at the end of this dispensation, according to the book
whose leaves sustain me while they gum my mouth with aloes,
purging recollections of the shores of my salvation —
where the palm trees sing hosanna in the harmattan wind —
I accept the fact of my irrelevance, the naïveté of my faith,
this self-indulgent journey like a transatlantic crossing by canoe.

Like a fleet of blazing galleons, Selassie's thunderclouds
will not appear above Manhattan on the eve of the millennium,
raining hail and brimstone on the worshippers of mammon.
At midnight dissonant dialects will be chiming in Times Square,
and the elders' watchful eyes will not be watered by the whiteness
of a phosphorescent stallion with a sterling-silver saddle,
thundering in the heavens on a branch of glimmering light.

In the mirror my reflection glares the truth of my disgrace —
a righteous rasta cabby, heavy in the chest, big in the neck,
dreadlocks like a rack of antlers, mangy buckskin cap,
I want to gun this Crown Victoria to a taxidermist's shop,
want to rass dis red and freeze myself in beams of arrowed light,
want to free me soul to dart across the range of possibility.

Outside, in the frost, hungry shoppers graze in herds, buffaloed in coats,
credit card numbers, scars, like keloids, branding them like steer.
Inside, the beaded steering wheel is cold against my fingers,
and my hands are dun and ashy like a pair of blighted palms.
At three-score years I have stopped bearing fruit.
The psalmist broke his promise. For all my ruminations
and my chalice-raising chants, Babylon has not fallen —
it was built too firmly on Manhattan's granite rock.
Wall Street has fallen to black bondsmen,
and hip-hop is the freedom song of youth as white as eggs;
and now that we are honored guests, the yolk must not be broken.

My heart cracks like a snare each time young poets "talk" revolution.
Like coupling "fuck" with "them" or "you" is a useful act of violence.
Like their beauty parlor locks will ever bolt them from employment.
Like their hair is really dreadful like the white man's bogey monster.
Frankenstein did not have time to glaze himself in gold,
Shelley stamped the fucker with more gordian concerns—nothing as
mirthful as shoes.

In three weeks my race will walk into another thousand years.
In a fortnight they will waddle into Christmas, then Kwanzaa—
a celebration cobbled from amnesia, stitched by a tongue
whose threads of language bind us to the Arabs,
our brothers who sold us into slavery like Joseph, the dreamer,
who kept his faith because his God was not just true but living.

Things fall apart. The center cannot hold. Gutted, I have fallen.

1.
Grandma is playing hide-and-seek
with the grandchildren
stuffed into hidey holes
stuffing giggles into cupped palms

"Ready or not, here I come . . ."

She knows exactly where to look
but delights in delay
they curl into the same spaces
in happier versions to the cowering shapes
her children fled into
as she screamed their names
leather belt whistling her delight in whipping
in mauling
in humiliating

Grandma is playing hide-and-seek
with the grandchildren
constructing emotions that skipped a generation
searching for the love her heavy hand
slapped from her own sons and daughters

Whose sons and daughters

now cocooned
into their parents' hidey holes
stuff giggles into cupped palms
trembling with excitement, not fear

When Grandma decides it's time to find then

unlike their parents
at the same size before them
they'll scream in delight, not pain

2.
Strange

conjugation
changes my universe

Brennie was
EV did
Mishka had

I knew

My father is
My mother does
My sister has

Strange

To be present
for these passing tense

he hasnt written any notes yet
hasnt understood any street signs or even the price of the rastaman
ital stew
he hasnt known the crypt
the way a man can say things to a woman without presence

he doesnt know silence
and he knows it so much more through seeing
and if it is believing
he is his own savior and sinner.

easier to absorb porn and cable . . .

arrg scritchy scratch.

he cannot leave a note for his wife if he chooses to kill himself
 nor can he leave a note if he chooses rebirth . . .

all he leaves are holes punched in his bathroom door
the remnant of rage toward his mother displaced
he leaves collections of ammunition,
assorted caliber barrels
 pins and hammers in separate packaging
he leaves spent shells beside seashells on Bull Bays black sand

and blood sips the edge of a creeping tide
where wild dogs gang an already dead man

he leaves red footprints on his grandmothers coconut-haired mat
 ejaculate on towels stuffed behind the toilet . . .
he pisses in the sink sometimes and knows that it is wrong
but just to defy everything for release . . .

he learned to read faces,
the shapes of clothing, bulges in waists,
 he learned to read intonation, learned to find a girls soul
stuck in her throat . . . coax it out from her mouth
and swallow it . . .

He was his own seeing dog
his own tap tap tapping stick . . .
blind mans vision
seeing & knowing everything from the source that is himself.
He is a dictionary,
a lexicon of personalized interpretations of letters words and phrases
heard and memorable,
sentences to hold on to, others to create,

but his lexicon does not align with the websters, wikipedia, oxfords,
it instead aligns with the potholes, orange peel, lime leaf tea and ackee
and saltfish
and if you ever taste how he spice down the nations national dish!
 brilliant young man, but his own self inflicted boa constrictor . . .

Calabash Writer's Workshop Fellow

I believe my children are the center of the universe.
I believe water can wash away worries.
That a baby sleeping on your chest is to be savored and sniffed.
I believe in long walks and long drives with no fixed route or destination.
I believe in holding hands,
sleeping late on Sunday mornings,
and walking in step.
I believe in eye contact between lovers and strangers.
I believe in crying while laughing and laughing while crying.
That being family doesn't mean you share blood.
It is always the pregnant woman's right to choose even when it's not fair to the man.
We should constantly strive for grace even though we may never achieve it.
Women got easy and men got lazy and that's a shame for both.
I believe in sunsets, moonsets, dolphins and rainbows.
I believe Usain Bolt running is a joy to behold.
I believe you can watch TV together while in two different countries.
I believe in dancing, fucking and making love,
and that it is best to fuck and make love to the same person.
I believe in driving fast listening to loud music on an open road.
No one should die alone.
Pedophiles should be executed.
I believe in redemption except for Roman Catholic priests who are pedophiles.
I believe organized religion has done more harm than good.
I believe that Islam is misunderstood.
Everyone should speak at least two languages.
Obama has brought hope.
Communication is the key to understanding.
I believe in stars in a woman's eyes,
multiple orgasms,
and oxytocin as my drug of choice.
I believe in imagination.
I believe in popcorn at the movies.

I believe in kissing, kissing and kissing.

I believe in toes touching.

I believe all women are by nature bisexual.

I believe strong women are looking for a stronger man.

That poetry is the highest form of writing.

That the smell of celluloid, ganja and sugarcane burning remind me of my father.

That all negative emotions stem from fear.

I believe we should listen to Bob Marley more often.

I believe that hormones and genes determine us.

I believe the true test of a person's character is what they do when no one is watching.

I believe the word *Love* is overused.

And *Like* is underrated.

I believe Facebook promotes a false sense of intimacy and community.

I believe in loyalty.

I believe that the man emerging from the bushes when your car breaks down in the middle of the night is coming to help not hurt.

I believe that happiness is a choice.

And if I am wrong
about any or all of the above
it doesn't really matter
because I also believe
in evolution,
transformation
and a woman's right to simply change her mind.

The houses are shut, the neighbors gone
to the burning field at the mangrove's edge,
where the heatstroke anthropologist writes
his prophecy in a wrenched tense:
"Their Gods . . . they've drowned."
All day I choke on the pages' knotted vines:
the totems will be covered, the Revivalists'
prayer poles, the rain woman's dance,
her rattle sticks beating the earth, until
the clothesline quivers like the Spanish
fly, pressed to a concrete block
by a boy, aiming his blunt needle.

The workers will return at dark, at the beetle's horn,
to the shack alley, to the rasps of sankeys
on the dead man's moth-meshed veranda;
they will gather for nine nights to the prophet's
rum-riddled call, with coco pods, mint bush,
cerasee, Bay Rum, Bible leaves and Phensic —
they will gnash teeth and groan epiphanies
with swaying bottle lamps over the fowl's blood
spilled on the ash, and on a body, with the dead's
tongue, warning all before morning. Frenetic,
without proper exegesis, I cut stone-cold
through the bush-lane home.

But the sugar-headed children will wander
the field at night, lost to the scavenging
green, eating the ripe flux of the land,
and then emptying their guts in the river
no longer worshipped, now a machine,
like the factory's tractors passing, loaded

with burnt canes, their foreheads white
with marl dust. Their eyes burn, gazing
at the half-yam moon—their tribe's
biography, a possession they cannot read.

They clatter away, children and tractors,
threading the coiled sleep that will not loosen
into the meager flash beyond suffering—
the light opening a book toward a simplicity
hard to achieve, though they are simple saints.
In the final dusk they head for the hill
holding up the sky, the shutterless, dozing shacks—
the hill they will rise to before work and play,
the hill will rise before tomorrow's dead.

DAT BUMPYHEAD GYAL *Joan Andrea Hutchinson*

*Written in 1996 in the aftermath of the furor created
when the writer wore a "black" Nubian knots hairstyle
(a.k.a. chiney bumps) to host a program on Jamaican TV*

Tell mi say mi nuh good enuff fi yuh TV screen
How mi offen yuh eyesight
Tell mi say mi a one black, ugly, bumpyhead gyal
An mi tell yuh, mi feelin right

Cuss mi say mi a one bootoo an mi nuh have nuh class
Trace mi, an galang rude
Tell mi say a educated woman should a know better
An mi tell yuh, mi feelin good

Yuh say mi hairstyle disgustin, chacka chacka an tan bad
An fayva sinting out a street
An say mi should a shame fi lef mi house tan so
An mi smile, mi feelin sweet

Yuh see, mi nuh fraid a mi owna self
Mi nuh shame a mi
Entime mi look inna di mirror mi love di smaddy
Weh mi see a look pan mi

Mi love her tick nappy hair an her broad face
Mi like her een an out a clothes
An bes of all mi love weh she tan up fi, an defen
An, a nuh pose she a pose

But serious, when yuh a go fall in love wid yuh
An leggo off a all a yuh fear
When yuh a go teck di time tell God tanks fi yuh life
Instead a fret bout hair

Caw ef it kinky, or straight, black or white
Transparent or opaque
Masa God meck everybody fi a special reason
An God doan meck mistake

But ef all yuh kyan do a criticize di Faada wuck
Den yuh life a go be salt
Becaw Him love wi an look after all a wi
Even when wi have nuff fault

So galang, call mi black an bumpyhead ef yuh waan
But meck sure yuh say t loud
Becaw di Creator love mi, an mi feel good fi be
Bumpyhead, black an proud

langtime lovah
mi mine run pan yu all di while
an mi membah how fus time
di two a wi come een—it did seem
like two shallow likkle snakin stream
mawchin mapless hapless a galang
tru di ruggid lanscape a di awt sang

an a soh wi did a gwaan
sohtil dat fateful day
awftah di pashan a di hurricane
furdah dan imaginaeshan ar dream
wi fine wiself lay-dung pan di same bedrack
flowin now togedah as wan stream
ridin sublime tru love lavish terrain
lush an green an brite awftah di rain
shimmarin wid glittahrin eyes
glowin in di glare a di smilin sun

langtime lovah
mi feel blue fi true wen mi tink bout yu
blue like di sky lingahrin pramis af rain
in di leakin lite in di hush af a evenin twilite
wen mi membah how fus time
di two a wi come een—it did seem
like a lang lang rivah dat is wide an deep

somtime wi woz silent like di langwidge a rackstone
somtime wi woodah sing wi rivah sang as wi a wine a galang
somtime wi jus cool an caam andah plenty shady tree
somtime sawfly lappin bamboo root as dem swing an sway
somtime cascadin carefree doun a steep gully bank

somtime turbulent in tempament wi flood wi bank
but weddah ebb ar flow tru rain tru drout
wi nevah stray far fram love rigid route

ole-time sweet-awt
up till now mi still cyaan andastan
ow wi get bag doun inna somuch silt an san
rackstone debri lag-jam
sohtil wi ad woz fi flow wi separet pawt
now traversin di tarrid terrain a love lanscape
runnin fram di polueshan af a cantrite awt
mi lang fi di marvelous miracle a hurricane
fi carry mi goh a meetin stream agen
lamentin mi saltid fate
sohmizin seh it too late

I made love to you, & it loomed there.
We sat on the small veranda of the cottage,
& listened hours to the sea talk.
I didn't have to look up to see if it was still there.
For days, it followed us along the polluted beaches
where the boys herded cows
& the girls danced for the boys,
to the moneychanger,
& then to the marketplace.
It went away when the ghost of my mother
found me sitting beneath a palm,
but it was in the van with us on a road trip to the country
as we zoomed past thatch houses.
It was definitely there when a few dollars
exchanged hands & we were hurried
through customs, past the guards.
I was standing in the airport in Amsterdam,
sipping a glass of red wine, half lost in van Gogh's
swarm of colors, & it was there, brooding in a corner.
I walked into the public toilet, thinking of W.E.B.
buried in a mausoleum, & all his books & papers
going to dust, & there it was, in that private moment,
the same image: obscene because it was built
to endure time, stronger than their houses & altars.
The seeds of melon. The seeds of okra in trade winds
headed to a new world. I walked back into the throng
of strangers, but it followed me. I could see the path
slaves traveled, & I knew when they first saw it
all their high gods knelt on the ground.
Why did I taste saltwater in my mouth?
We stood in line for another plane,
& when the plane rose over the city,

I knew it was there, crossing the Atlantic.
Not a feeling, but a longing. I was in Accra
again, gazing up at the vaulted cathedral ceiling
of the compound. I could see the ships at dusk
rising out of the lull of Amazing Grace, cresting
the waves. The governor stood on his balcony,
holding a sword, pointing to a woman
in the courtyard, saying, That one.
Bring me that tall, ample wench.
Enslaved hands dragged her to the center,
then they threw buckets of water on her,
but she tried to fight. They penned her to the ground.
She was crying. They prodded her up the stairs. One step,
& then another. Oh, yeah, she still had some fight in her,
but the governor's power was absolute. He said:
There's a tyranny of language in my fluted bones.
There's poetry on every page of the good book.
There's God's work to be done in a forsaken land.
There's a whole tribe in this one, but I'll break them
before they're in the womb, before they're conceived,
before they're even thought of. Come, up here,
don't be afraid, up here to the governor's quarters,
up here where laws are made. I haven't delivered
the head of Pompey or John the Baptist
on a big silver tray, but I own your past,
present, & future. You're not like the others.
You're special. Breasts tender as ripest pears.
I'll break you with fists & cat-o'-nine.
I'll thoroughly break you, head to feet,
but sister I'll break you most dearly
with sweet words.

i live city center
on the inner edge
of the west side of town
walking distance from the tracks
that circle trains in and out
of scared suburbia

little more than a block
away from me
espresso or painted buddhas
milled soap or hand-blown glass
vendors hawk their wares
behind big plate-glass windows

still, i have found empty
bullet casings in the dirt
while planting my pole beans
and more than once been startled
by smoke rising from a glass pipe
as the shadow of a man crouches
in between the garbage bin and iron gate
sucking on desperate illusions of joy

last night a bass line
bent around the housing complex
reshaping bay windows
making them shudder and creak

and whatever music
swam inside that moment
was consumed by the sirens that quickly
circled the block defining where their

civil society ended and our dark
and therefore dangerous hood began

i try to hold onto the band of purple
that edged the heron's wings
as she rose soft in the green of a connecticut evening
the moon rising full and heavy in star-rich skies
the birds singing darkness and dawn outside my window
the gypsy moths taunting me on my evening walks
the river bathing my feet while cooling my thoughts

but there are more than miles between there and here
and more than time between then and now

Cruising up the Waltham
so hard to overstand
what's the Plan? and who's the man?
and who shot ya? Damn!
so hard to forget can't correct the past
knowing that time waits for no man
and it flies so fast
briefly believe me
ash to ash dust to dust
cemeteries never full
more time it seems as if
the graveyard waits for us.
how could one escape the fate
of a life lived wrong?
could i refuse to kill and still stay strong?
could i meditate keep my mind state
without hits from the chalice or bong?
will I remember you in the years
after you're gone?
or will i be the trigga nigga
when it's time to put it on?
easy like Sunday morn
but too many mourn
living life insane like children
of the corn
every day a man die every day
a youth is born
the cycle of life it goes
on and on and on and on
the Most High swore
that His words would never pass
like heaven and Earth

so I look at my child since the day of her Birth
and realize in her eyes what life is worth
and dash whey certain tings that we was told at first
like we were born in sin, being black is a curse
I picture your coffin in the back of a hearse
knowing you was a cat whenever powder, nurse or pet
O.G. vet, who posed a deadly threat
so they gave you five shots to the chest and neck
now who's to protect
your woman? your child?
as your body disappear up the Styx
way past the Nile
and as I shed my tears I can't suppress my smile
should I laugh or cry? live or die?
heaven or hell who can tell?
same place, or different venue
a luta continua, the struggle continues, the struggle continues
the struggle continues.
we must conquer. no doubt.

DIS POEM

Mutabaruka

---

dis poem
shall speak of the wretched sea
that washed ships to these shores
of mothers cryin for their young
swallowed up by the sea
dis poem shall say nothin new
dis poem shall speak of time
time unlimited time undefined
dis poem shall call names
names like lumumba kenyatta nkrumah
hannibal akhenaton malcolm garvey
haile selassie
dis poem is vexed about apartheid rascism fascism
the ku klux klan riots in brixton atlanta jim jones
dis poem is revoltin against 1st world 2nd world
3rd world division man made decision.
dis poem is like all the rest
dis poem will not be amongst great literary works
will not be recited by poetry enthusiasts
will not be quoted by politicians nor men of religion
dis poem is knives bombs guns blood fire
blazin for freedom
yes dis poem is a drum
ashanti mau mau ibo yoruba nyahbingi warriors
uhuru uhuru
uhuru namibia
uhuru soweto
uhuru afrika
dis poem will not change things
dis poem need to be changed
dis poem is a rebirth of a people
arizin awakin understandin

dis poem speak is speakin have spoken
dis poem shall continue even when poets have stopped writin
dis poem shall survive u me it shall linger in history
in your mind
in time forever
dis poem is time only time will tell
dis poem is still not written
dis poem has no poet
dis poem is just a part of the story
his-story her-story our-story the story still untold
dis poem is now ringin talkin irritatin
makin u want to stop it
but dis poem will not stop
dis poem is long cannot be short
dis poem cannot be tamed cannot be blamed
the story is still not told about dis poem
dis poem is old new
dis poem was copied from the bible your prayer book
playboy magazine the n.y. times readers digest
the c.i.a. files the k.g.b. files
dis poem is no secret
dis poem shall be called boring stupid senseless
dis poem is watchin u tryin to make sense from dis poem
dis poem is messin up your brains
makin u want to stop listenin to dis poem
but u shall not stop listenin to dis poem
u need to know what will be said next in dis poem
dis poem shall disappoint u
because
dis poem is to be continued in your mind in your mind
in your mind your mind

THE CINNAMON PEELER *Michael Ondaatje*

If I were a cinnamon peeler
I would ride your bed
and leave the yellow bark dust
on your pillow.

Your breasts and shoulders would reek
you could never walk through markets
without the profession of my fingers
floating over you. The blind would
stumble certain of whom they approached
though you might bathe
under rain gutters, monsoon.

Here on the upper thigh
at this smooth pasture
neighbor to your hair
or the crease
that cuts your back. This ankle.
You will be known among strangers
as the cinnamon peeler's wife.

I could hardly glance at you
before marriage
never touch you
—your keen-nosed mother, your rough brothers.
I buried my hands
in saffron, disguised them
over smoking tar,
helped the honey gatherers . . .

When we swam once
I touched you in water

and our bodies remained free,
you could hold me and be blind of smell.
You climbed the bank and said

    this is how you touch other women
the grasscutter's wife, the lime burner's daughter.
And you searched your arms
for the missing perfume.

    and knew

    what good is it
to be the lime burner's daughter
left with no trace
as if not spoken to in an act of love
as if wounded without the pleasure of scar.

You touched
your belly to my hands
in the dry air and said
I am the cinnamon
peeler's wife. Smell me.

"I don't believe in global warming . . ."

but the Atlantic warms
to storms
becoming hurricanes
that rush past South
to North America
swiping
the islands
in between
washing them clean
then on to maiming Cuba
blow away Florida
Florida
Florida

past that coast inland
to Galveston
believe me
even to Richmond
et cetera
et cetera . . .

"I do not see the HIV and AIDS connection . . ."

but women one in ten
die leaving babies
babies
babies
wards to bankrupt states . . .

Where leaders are not wise
the people (literally) perish

That wise man Uncle Nketia
come from Ghana tell us how
the music teacher (Euro)
teaching Afro children
eight-note scales
"there's nothing else"
had said
and Afro children
knowing polyrhythms
smiling sang in Euro rhythm
up and down
the eight-note scale

"the teacher is himself a fool
the teacher is himself a fool!"

"The only thing they can do is behead people"

Busha Bush intones
touching his own head
make sure it still there
what does he mean?

and unsuspecting
from the
Furious Flower floor
some bright black fellow
writing poetry
counter claims
low, deep, ironic
"they had to go to Bosnia

to find out
bout ethnic cleansing
but terrorism
never new to us
our brothers lynched
schoolchildren burned
each day a struggle just to be

If you be Black."

> *But they told me a man should be faithful and walk*
> *When not able and fight till the end . . .*
> —Michael Jackson, "Will You Be There"

To make of the heart-   song. Each pump
/counterpoint sound signaling your own
steel town thrum. Can you feel it? Bass
and bass again; but no thrum alone. Black folk know

there's no soliloquy in that downbeat. Each true
heart wants to speak, to be starting something joyfilled.
To be rockin-robin, double-dutch stunned with joy
to be a boy again, a sweet sparkling boy.

And his sequined hand, pulls
all radiance to the chest, against which
we count out the time, mimic the toe,
the heel, the hip, the luminous hip up and up and
oh the thrust,
the scream we knew we never understood.
To make of the skin; flag of tatters, each flap
a snap heel, a broken string in your father's guitar.
Each bloody thin strip we pulled, we wore
like our own red leather and we watched
from the corners of our eyes. We loved you
too silently. We rode you from that chitlin circuit
to this crazy circus of skin.

To make for the body a cortege of train cars,
a box of remains, the shaking shoulders of grief.
Bubblegum souls we hum your *na na na na na na na*
under breath. We watch for the light

as our workday trains rush the bridges, watch
for the gleam of sun on blacktop, on the gray blue
table of oceans, watch for our spotlight (*which
we believe might be kinder*) to come.

To shift each heart which occupies a small,
plain room; hearts of spill and backstreet,
hearts of island breeze and footpath, of teeming city
with babylonian tongue until each must twirl,
hum, sing, raise hand, sing *Ma ma se Ma* sing,
rejoice, sing, dance that body lifted unto god
to make of the tongue one dazzling silver key,
miracle scream, lyric cry. To make of the throat
giddy singing and incandescent glory.

To make of a plain pelvic bone the particular question
I've asked since I was a girl. To make of the mirror
a hard place to gaze without flinching. To make
of my mirror my young body dancing and of my body?
—to make it dance—still.

To make of change our credible hope and of your
heart- Song.

How every pressing vein in this optimistic
heart reaches out out, every chamber of the thing
believes someone is listening. The body resists fade.
The spectacle resents reflection. Can't find
no kind flashbulb, no unsparing spot in which to pool,
to rest, and we each testify:

This heart, this one weary/love sick/skin sore heart
is the song that has unfolded our many tongues.

Written for a collaboration with the Foundry Theatre

Section 1.

Though I might seem familiar, I'm not who you think I am.
I have no personal story to tell. If you feel involved it is not
because of me. Identity is time passing. Every moment of
what we call life is life in the shadow of choice, some fact of
your consciousness hesitating before me.

Are you wondering why we're here? Where we're going?
When we get there will you think, This is nice. This is new.
This is old. This is urban. These are the real people. These are
the other people. This is the old New York . . . whatever. You
shouldn't think.

Listen, let's say this is the type of tour where we travel from
place to place entering what is. Let's say we are unnecessary
to the streets we will travel though. Let's say nothing will
happen beyond what is happening since you and I both know
nothing usually happens.

Still, I know you want to negotiate this time between us. You
want to understand your freedoms and "unfreedoms" in relation
to me. But there will be no speaking to me, no conversing, no
negotiating.

I understand your need for intimacy. You want to feel in-
timate with me so you can define yourself against me. You
want to be able to say, I know you; I feel as you do; I see you.
But doesn't this type of intimacy always end up with someone
being fucked? I am not going to let you be cruel to me.

There is however one thing about me that I cannot keep from you. Once we have crossed this bridge, once the Harlem River flows beneath us, once Mary, our bus driver, says, We are entering the Bronx, what you look at will look back at you.

Once you see me I will have seen you, and an intimacy, despite everything, will commence. Then you will want me to convince you, and I will want to convince you (and myself) of my beauty. Then everything, this intimacy everyone craves, will depend on what definition of beauty controls our seeing.

Section 4.

I tell you all this because I want to make being here all that matters. I want our vehicular flow, the road construction, all accidents and delays to be part of what constitutes here.

A long time ago, before Jesus, someone said, You need to be responsible for your own passage, all this life, all this living. Congestion will be, is, no matter how much we try to facilitate movement, no matter how much signage directs us.

Did you know that the ideal cruising speed is thirty miles per hour? Speed limits are just one example of a Traffic Calming Measure that engineers have come up with. Even they realize our hearts race though we sit still.

Somewhere
in the deepest darkest regions
there is a tribe of women
who speak a language
no man understands.

I listen to their walking

The movement
hunched over always,
backward, knotted.
That body another time.
Bent strange
exaggerating everything.

The moon made red
sweet the mercurial glow
of acid spit.

From the root they pull up weeds
blow the wet smell of lilacs
onto bruised orchards
grow crops in balding fields
Keep quiet until cancers heal.

Always stealing time
from a peaceful place
while repeating wavering footsteps
and swatting things away
from a wandering eye.

A breast.
A gash.
A tone.
A tongue
of shapeless light.

The tribal pose
of rebuke
in cool
half cocked smiles
and smoke.

Out-living language all together.

Without dispute
these are
the tallest trees . . .

The envy of years.

Women everywhere
speak a language
they can only dance
twelve times before
the earth is fully settled.

Just whistling at white legs once
upon a time could get a black man
torn apart by some giddy mob tipsy
with their fair skin and cold beer—
and there'd be picnics while he swung
and some singing in the round.

But back then is not now, and the future
is a ditty I hum to myself the way
a child might whistle Dixie just to keep
from hearing what teethes in the dark,
and for most of my life I have lived there:
belonging and not belonging to America—

this fat animal shape on the globe
where white people have done so much
to so many and get "pretty tired of hearing
about it." I'm not trying to be mean.
I've got some white blood in my veins,
and really, *whiteness* is just a shadow

of its former self, but still, I'm kinda
scared, confused about what to do
with History while I'm sitting in a park
in Virginia holding a white woman's hand.
I never want to think being American
is impossible, but the truth is

some silly mothafuckas still fly
Confederate flags and maybe it's all
too much for any one man. I would like
to say she smiles a smile that locks

the door on grief, that her legs
could make a new priest pause, that

what is unsaid between us—in the meeting
of our complicated skins—is itself
a word: felt but never defined,
exactly like Time, the way it
shoves everybody forward, then
leaves all of us way behind.

I remember kissing Karen Stickney
in *kidneygarden*, her hair vaselined and wavy,
her buttery brown cheek damp against my lips
how, for the rest of the day, my little brain whistled
like a Wiffle ball, though the teacher did make me
stay after school. I told Karen I would save her

if she fell down a hill—and I meant it,
as much as a five-year-old can. Now, fifty years
deep into this, that's mostly what I'm looking for:
a touch of daylight with someone who can turn me
away from the tilt of my own nervous humming.

But what can I say to the black woman
who gives me that hard stare, who cannot hear
my heart crooning, *Of course, I love sistas,*
but isn't everybody beautiful?
In so many ways, the blood *is* still wet
on the lash and I see black bodies

every day pressed into capital—army, navy,
NBA, NFL—and who gets to live inside them

lovely new prisons? It must be a riddle
being white, knowing and not knowing what's
what: afraid of the dark citizens but so in love
with that funky music. Even this

slyly freckled woman who lightly squeezes my hand,
whose white skin hides her own hard story,
breathes an air I can't quite fit into my lungs,
though we groove to Parliament,
and she throws her hips hard enough
to shake the centuries loose.

I want to believe love can be big enough
to beat back all the bad news, and today,
I don't think I do, but maybe I think too much,

and a touch of lips *is* bigger than History,
and where I am, this present tense, is just a song
that's really over by the time it begins.

To Chrystos

come
to the water
and I will
hold you
bathe
your embattled body
wash your bludgeoned spirit
splash healing droplets
on your face
its beauty marred
sores left
by curse word venom
take my tongue
to these wounds
cleanse them
lance them
drain the hateful pus

come
to the water
your breath
fetid
with garroted truths
you fear to tell
and i will kiss you
my lips
engulf
you whole
my saliva will serve as
balm
to cancerous cankers

loosen your tongue
give you
voice
to affirm your life
set you to singing

come
to the water
touch
my raw body
an exposed nerve
your hands
massage my insides
extract gangrene
from my veins
left by
hypodermic
phobias and hate
your fingers
fill holes
made by derision
apathy
fair-weather
friends and family

come
to the water
let us
prepare potions
spiritual elixirs
pride tonics
emetics to vent the spleen

shed tears
to replenish the pool
find other
bodies broken
souls shattered
eyes put out
spirits splintered
lead them
to the water
to bathe in love
and be healed.

Calabash Writer's Workshop Fellow

XL

In Memoriam, John Hearne

Whatever the parish, cored in cobalt green,
the breadfruit's broad, open palm, coralita
embroidering the full hedges, St. Elizabeth, Trelawny
sounding like perpetual spring pouring a liter
of chilled white wine, slopes of raw red dirt,
I think of him now as his own phantom walking
along a cool mountain road with his white panama
and the martial, bristling moustache, his tawny
skin, howling at his own puns, *friend or enema*;
alone on his own road as the car makes a turn
and he is gone, gone without turning his head
to acknowledge our emerald friendship, I mean John Hearne,
his prose rustling from a tall cedar. He heard
his sentences rustle like branches, the hidden
noise of spring constant under mountain fern
walking straight as a gift that did what it was bidden,
to praise how a horse crosses a meadow, un-ridden,
but purposefully, pausing to whinny and snort,
the sweat sheen on it, deep in remembering thought.

XLI

For Lorna Goodison

This prose has the gait of a mule urged up a mountain road,
a slope with wild strawberries; yes, strawberries grow there,
and pines also flourish native trees from abroad,
and coffee-bush shining in the crisp blue air
fanning the thighs of the mountains. Pernicious ginger
startles around corners and crushed lime
leaves its memory on thumb and third finger,
each page has the freshness of girlhood's time,
when by a meager brook the white scream
of an egret beats with the same rhythm as crows
circling invisible carrion in their wide dreams;
commas sprout like thorn bush alongside this curved prose
descending into some village named Harvey River
whose fences are Protestant. A fine Presbyterian
drizzle blesses each pen with its wooden steeple over
baking zinc roofs. Adjectives are modestly raised in this terrain,
this side-saddle prose on its way to the dressmaker
passes small fretwork balconies, drying clothes
in a yard smelling of Monday; this prose
has the sudden smell of a gust of fragrant rain
on scorching asphalt from the hazed hills of Jamaica.

PART IV:
EXTRA LARGE

CALABASH BAY

BIRTHPLACE
(WITH BURIED STONES)

Meena Alexander

I.

In the absence of reliable ghosts I made aria,
Coughing into emptiness, and it came,

A west wind from the plains with its arbitrary arsenal:
Torn sails from the Ganga River,

Bits of spurned silk,
Strips of jute to be fashioned into lines,

What words stake — sentence and make believe,
A lyric summoning.

II.

I came into this world in an Allahabad hospital
Close to a smelly cow pasture.

I was brought to a barracks with white walls
And corrugated tin roof

Beside a Civil Aviation Training Center
— In World War II officers were docketed there —

I heard the twang of propellers,
Jets pumping hot whorls of air

Heaven bent,
Blessing my first home.

III.
In an open doorway, in half darkness,
I see a young woman standing.

Her breasts are swollen with milk.
She is transfixed, staring at a man,

His hair gleaming with sweat,
Trousers rolled up,

Stepping off his bicycle.
Mustard bloom catches in his shirt.

I do not know what she says to him,
Or he to her, all that is utterly beyond me.

Their infant once a clot of blood
Is spectral still.

Behind this family are vessels of brass
Dotted with saffron,

The trunk of a mango tree chopped into bits,
Ready to be burnt at the household fire.

IV.
Through the portals of that larger chaos,
What we can scarcely conceive of in our minds—

We'd rather think of starry nights with biting flames
Trapped inside tree trunks, a wellspring of desire

Igniting men and gods,
A lava storm where butterflies dance—

Comes bloodletting at the borders,
Severed tongues, riots in the capital,

The unspeakable hurt of history:
So the river Ganga pours into the sea.

V.
In aftermath—the elements of vocal awakening:
Crud, spittle, snot, menstrual blistering,

Also infant steps, a child's hunger, a woman's rage
At the entrance to a kitchen,

Her hands picking up vegetable shavings, chicken bones,
Gold tossed from an ancestral keep.

All this flows in me as mottled memory,
Mixed with syllables of sweat, gashed syntax,

Strands of burst bone in river sand,
Beside the buried stones of Saraswati Koop,

Well of mystic sky-water where swans
Dip their throats and come out dreaming.

Marooned, tenantless, deserted. Desolation castaway, aban-
doned in the world. They was, is, wandered, wanders as spirits
who dead cut, banished, seclude, refuse, shut the door, derelict,
relinquished, apart. More words she has left them. Cast behind.
From time to time they sit on someone's bed or speak to some-
one in the ear and that is why someone steps out of rhythm; that
is why someone drinks liquor or trips or shuts or opens a door
out of nowhere. All unavailable to themselves, open to the world,
cut in air. They disinherit answers. They owe, own nothing. They
whisper every so often and hear their own music in churches,
restaurants, hallways, all paths, between fingers and lips, between
cars and precipices, and the weight of themselves in doorways, on
the legs of true hipsters, guitars and bones for soup, veins.

And it doesn't matter where in the world, this spirit is no citi-
zen, no national, no one who is christened, no sex, this spirit is
washed of all this lading, bag and baggage, jhaji bundle, georgie
bindle, lock stock, knapsack, and barrel, and only holds its own
weight which is nothing, which is memoryless and tough with
remembrances, heavy with lightness, aching with grins. They
wander as if they have no century, as if they can bound time, as
if they can sit in a café in Brugge just as soon as smoke grass in
Tucson, Arizona, and chew coca in the high Andes for coldness.

Pays for everything this one, hitchhikes, dies in car accidents,
dresses in Hugo Boss and sings ballads in Catholic churches,
underwater rum shops. This is a high-wire spirit laden with an-
chors coming in to land, devoluting heirlooms, parcels, movable
of nips, cuts, open secrets of foundlings, babes, ignitions, strips
of water, cupfuls of land, real estates of ocean floors and steam-
ing asphalt streets, meat of trees and lemons, bites of Commu-
nion bread and chunks of sky, subdivisions of stories.

These spirits are tenants of nothing jointly, temporary inheritors of pages 276 and 277 of an old paleology. They sometimes hold a life like a meeting in a detention camp, like a settlement without a stone or stick, like dirty shelves, like a gag in the mouth. Their dry goods are all eaten up already and their hunger is tenacious. This spirit doubling and quadrupling, resuming, skipping stairs and breathing elevators, is possessed with uncommunicated undone plots; consignments of compasses whose directions tilt, skid off known maps, details skitter off like crabs. This spirit abandoned by all mothers, fathers, all known progenitors, rents rooms that disappear in its slate stone wise faces. These people un-people, de-people until they jump overboard, hijack buildings and planes. They disinhabit unvisited walls. They unfriend friends in rye and beer and homemade wine and forties.

She undwells solitudes, liquors' wildernesses. This drunk says anything, cast away in his foot ship, retired from the world. This whisperer, sprawler, mincer, deaconess, soldier is marooning, is hungering, is unknowing. This one in the suit is a litigant in another hearing gone in the world. This spirit inhaling cigarettes is a chain along a thousand glistening moss harbors and spends nights brooding and days brooding and afternoons watching the sea even at places with no harbors and no sea. This one is gone, cast off and wandering willfully. This is intention as well as throwaway. This is deliberate and left. Slipstream and sailing. Deluge. These wander anywhere, clipping shirttails and hems and buying shoes and vomiting. These shake with dispossession and bargain, then change their minds. They get trapped in houses one minute, just as anybody can, and the next they break doorways and sit in company mixing up the talk with crude honesty and lies. Whatever is offered or ceded is not the thing,

not enough, cannot grant their easement, passports to unknow-
ing everything.

This spirit's only conveyance is each morning, breath, depar-
tures of any kind, tapers, sheets of anything, paper, cloth, rain,
ice, spittle, glass. It likes blue and fireflies. Its face is limpid.
It has the shakes, which is how it rests and rests cutting oval
shells of borders with jagged smooth turns. It is an oyster leav-
ing pearl. These spirits have lived in any given year following
the disaster, in any given place. They have visited shutters and
doors and thermal glass windows looking for themselves. They
are a prism of endless shimmering color. If you sit with them
they burn and blister. They are bony with hope, muscular with
grief possession.

Marooned on salted highways, in high grass, on lumpy beds,
in squares with lights, in knowledge plantations and cunning
bridges grasping two cities at the same time. Marooned in the
mouth where things escape before they are said, are useless
before they are given or echo. Marooned in realms of drift, mas-
sacres of doubt, implications. Marooned where the body burns
with longing for everything and nothing, where it circles unable
to escape a single century; tenements and restagings of alien,
new landings. Marooned in outcropping, up-crops of cities
already abandoned for outposts in suburbs. Deserted in the fra-
gility of concrete rooms, the chalked clammy dust of dry walls,
the rot of sewer pipes and the blanket of city grates.

Marooned in music, dark nightclubs of weeping, in never-
sufficient verses, uncommunicated sentences, strict tears, in
copper throats. Where days are prisons this spirit is a tenant.

She moves along incognito on foot, retreating into unknowing, retreating into always orphanages, dew light, paradise, eclipses, bruised skies, atomic stars, an undeviating ever.

So if now and then they slump on beds in exhaustion it is hallowed pain. If they sink in the ear it is subversions that change their minds even before they are deployed, unexpected architectures of ambivalent longing, cargoes of wilderness. It is their solitudes' wet desolations. If they finger a string across a piece of wood and a tremolo attacks a room, toccata erupt, coloratura saturate the walls, it is their lost and found dereliction. If virtuosity eludes them, relinquishes them, cast away to themselves only, gaping limbs and topographies, it is just as much spiritoso, madrigal, mute chirping, ululating twilight unvisiting.

It is now and she, they whisper in Walkmans, in cities' streets with two million people gazing at advertisements. It is now and he, they run his fingers over a mustache flicking frost away, breathing mist like a horse. Cities and public squares and public places corral their gifts of imagined suns and imagined families, where they would have been and who they might have been and when. Cities make them pause and wonder at what they might have thought had it been ever, and had it been dew light and had it been some other shore, and had it been time in their own time when now they are out of step with themselves as spirits are. Electric lights and neon and cars' metal humming convince them of cultivated gateways and generations of water, of necessities they cannot put back together. Their coherence is incoherence, provocations of scars and knives and paradise, of tumbling wooden rivers and liquid hills.

Is just a hard back
with a soft bitter middle

denoting a gathering of some books

and a collection of their writers
by an arbitrary sea

nobody ever hear of such a thing
in the West Indies turned Caribbean

colonial and rigid
readings have always been difficult for those of us
with no poetry of note—at least among the lighter class of folks

the people's poems have always been hard to hear

tough to bear the yawp of a hungry child
embedded in a pleasant rhyme
turned clever to make you split your insides

out damned spot

the poor have always cleaned for Jamaica
for England
even America—land of free and whatnot—poor people still on them knees

but this talk is not about global things
this riff is really about a soft spot of sand
rocks jutting boastful from the water

———————

manish water and short stories
curry goat and biographies
jerk chicken and a few haiku

what would you do in a place of words
woven idyllic into breezy afternoons

rooms let by the villagers
night walking and early morning talks with strangers
on the beach
mangoes and madness

love and the making of things pretty enough to photograph

some things we left unrecorded
memory is all we desired from those moments

Jamaica/with all your turbulence
your violent letting of my blood inking these stories

inside the bitter flesh of this hardback calabash

I am more than the lesbian
the loud-mouth-vagina-screaming-barefoot woman

deep in the center

lives a girl grieving an island
the dew and the dust
the plantains and perpetual posturing of my people

I am growing easier with our history
speaking my truths
to your power

I am nothing if I am not Jamaican

hard back
with the soft bitter middle
good for carrying water

for keeping food warm
or cool
depending on the dish you craving

you are what you is
my grandmother used to say
cane don't come without bump

and I am learning to love
the rough rise of where I come from
the sweet walk between points of difficulty

therein
lies the sugar
the molasses

the thick bitter of what could both kill and cure you

but no matter what ails you/the sea
could always wash things away

clean/clean

just mutter two words
make them rhyme
rinse them in the water
and leave the rest to time

soon
the jutting rocks will smooth
the roaring waves will quiet

leaving only the bittersweet echo
of a once upon a lyme

If I'm a criminal for advocating that people have the right to defend themselves
and fight for what they deserve—then I hope I'm always known as a criminal.
—Robert F. Williams, President of NAACP, Monroe, N.C., 1954

The father leads her by the arm for her first lesson.
They head behind the house past the prayer trees,

beyond the woods,
back back of the shed,
into the old hush hush air
where prayer and camp meeting
rose like jasmine vine,
back in the black code days.

Their walk sideways, through the fall sun,
into the old old woods, has been written
by carpenter pencil on the wide-block
insurance calendar for fifteen years,

since the day the midwife left behind
one extra long, glistening, brown taffy baby,
rolled, safe & center,
of the white white sheet.

The escort father moves with one hand
on his Smith & Wesson (his German
luger sleeps deep in his waistband)
and one hand gentling her shooting arm
with every step, never pulling.
Her head high, eyes low low,
her breath full of one last useless resist;

Why I have to do what she do?

At the speckled breathy chicken wire
of a door stands the one afraid of heights,
who can blow blow the x out the Maxwell House
can, who knows that nothing that comes
in twos, on her, was ever ever taught to squint.

The mother-markswoman, dressed
in cotton smock and brogans, stares
at the leaving backsides of the two she
would jump out of any airplane for.
When she practices and shoots the eyes
off a carpet beetle she tends to rise,
but she cannot swim, fly, leave land
or ground, with ease.

Years later strangers will arrive at her door
and try try to interview her for their
Black People Who Refused to Join King
documentary. She will announce at the same
breathy chicken wire of a door to the black
black eye of the camera:

What goes on in the backwoods —
stays on in the backwoods,

turning back to her pots
with nary a sound, her trigger finger
wet and soapy, content for now to coax
the egg & cheese off a casserole dish.

For now she stops her kitchen work
but not her kitchen worry worry. She has

just heard the first pulse of thunder break.
Her ears stretch and preen the bright
sun and half-mile of trees out into the field.
She closes her eyes, hoping to see the spot
where her two honey buns are walking even
before their feet feet reach the fault lines there.

Her brown hands covered in twice sifted
paprika & goose flour twitch.

The morning has her mindless & stuttering,
forgetting her hurricane of work ahead.
She touches for the itch near her nose.
A speckle of whitish wheat will dot her
face there until he returns. The hands of
the husband, not even fully off the copper
knob, will reach, sweetly, for her dark
gingerbread of face, for the poppy of white
that only he will notice strangely there.

She will never know the origin of this
errant bloom of dusty white. She will only
remember that he returned to her, found
something out of place, on her, and fixed it.
Just like the time before and the times times ahead.

How'd she do?
She'll ask.

Fruit don't run from where it falls.
He'll answer.

Back in the kitchen her hands rest on the
red cake bowl, the fatty chicken thighs her
daughter favors, bob and dive, dive and bob,
like overweight synchronized swimmers;
the Berlin Olympics, 1936. Jesse had already
won. Hitler had begun to bite at the skin
of his pearl white fists. Tanned with fresh
garlic the thighs stretch into a colored Swan
Lake, bubbling up & down, from a full night's
practice-sleep, inside the silky clabber of milk
butter. The greens, settled and woozy, collapse
their leathery skins inside a bog of Nile pot liquor.

At the knotty, rusty screen, the mother,
who can shoot the first and second s
from out the middle middle of grasshopper,
without endangering the grass or the hop hop,
stares into the field of yellowing pine,
for sign of insect life or other other.

Gunpowder lifts every tree into the air,
cabbage-colored cicadas lickity split from a pie
that has been cut, and they the only lucky life
released. Her wide toes widen more on the
wooden threshold, shaved three times, with
three different-sized scythes, over three weeks.
Her steel wool heels bare down down on the
well-buttered heart pine boards, and take the
wood like cornbread poured out on a hot griddle,

behind her
the pig iron smokes.

On the way from and to All Saints Sunday school
        girl passed their meetings; parson said they were
            nothing but uncouth heathen un-Christian pagans.

Still she was moved so by their loose limb moves
        faces oiled-up, eyeballs rolled way back in socket
            made poem's later talk of inward eye spell sense.

Desire rose in her to echo their loud glory-trumpet
        shouts, she'd swallow hard when bidden to stand
            stock still and mechanical pipe hymns from a pew.

Or kneel to be always led in prayer by the minister
        who is remembered not for uplifting sermons, just
            for how he'd prostrated himself in the center aisle

to demonstrate the prone position of that traveler
        who had fallen among thieves; the man redeemed
            by a good Samaritan; that was the same clergyman

who'd rebuked her, said she was prone to causing
        commotions whenever she entered Sunday school.
            So she tried thereafter to speak softly so and train

her eyes upon the crucifix of a black Christ cut
        and carved from a struck-by-lightning ebony tree
            to whom she squeezed out petitions: O Dear Lord

Do Lord, help me never more to cause commotions.
        May I grow into a woman pure chaste virtuous
            as the Blessed Virgin, and not a harlot like Jezebel.

On the way home the girl witnessed this drama:
   A band of Africans jumping poco in the streets
      and a church mother in the grip of the paraclete.

It pitched her down flat, ripped off her tie head
     wiped it across the concrete, hiked her white gown
        to expose shine thighs that scissored and cut

clean the slipknot that bound spirit to sense.
     The girl stood there amazed in her Sunday dress,
       stood in her burnished black shoes and wondered

that her white dress was not more a bridal gown
    was girl's concern as she received first communion.
       Confirmed, girl felt nothing, not the merest breath

the Holy Spirit blew right past her at the rail
     to anoint with a kiss the high brow of good girl
       who did not in secret aspire to be Lavern Baker.

O to be a a torch singer denizen of smoky places,
     dolled up in ruched satin gowns, bee stung lips
       stained ruby red by Max Factor, ah the slow burn

siren style of exquisite evening attire, the affect
     of set struck pose so languid yet set to run race
       of hard running women of the racehorse ankles,

dreamy eyes veiled half closed by cigarette smoke.
     O to make moan about the man done gone and left
       a lady at daybreak to tell heartache good morning.

This way of being she came by honestly; by books,
            her father—player of instruments wind and string—
                        and six brothers who spun vinyl: 78   33 1/3   45.

Sixteen, and her ambition was to be a big woman.
                  To perform in concert with Sarah Ella Billie Dinah
                        To wonder like them at whereabouts of loverman,

where O where can you be, loverman or paraclete?
                  In the presence of all the Saints she petitions him:
                        Come o come on wings and let me feel something.

Not song it seems but sweetheart of song; poetry
            for certain it came on those wings viewless, none
                        not even she saw it turn her from hankering after

the scorch way of torch singers, long slow burning.
                  For she had set her gaze on Billie Holiday's cream
                        gardenias brought fresh by night blooming admirers.

            small blues for Billie's gardenia

                        mixed signals sent
                        scent sensual
                        yet nunlike

                        wide open
                        light bloom
                        worn heart side

REGGAE RANT ❧ *Kendel Hippolyte*

For Kamau Brathwaite

Doom
> *!Scatter*

Doom
> *!Scatter*

Doom   **Doom**   **Doom**   **Doom**   **Doom**
> *!Scatter*   *!Scatter*   *!Scatter*   *!Scatter*

When the scrabbling city crawls nightways in penultimate light,
and the night wind is whorish, skirting around corners, twitching with a
hiss down alleys,
the sound of the beast approaching
starts a backwash in the drains, stirs the unmoving muck in the canals
which had begun as rivers
and crosses narrowing bridges crouched over our waste
to come to bodyslam us down, back down, onto the bass ground of our selves

Doom   **Doom**   **Doom**   **Doom**   **Doom**

claws strumming in a sweet, raking viciousness, eyelids down to the groin,
groin back again up to the eyelids

> *!Scatter*   *!Scatter*   *!Scatter*   *!Scatter*

Friday evening, the twilight, something wrings out dry the bleeding gauze-
and-lint sky over us
flicking the drops of blood-flecked light in scattering gouts over the city,
over the heads of high school kids starting to herd, to massive
on the stomping grounds of corners,
and as the last drops of darklight fall spattering on their heads, a lowering
swell of tongues babels upward
an anti-Pentecostal unholy ghostly outpouring of jagged wordsong, infernal
music

thud/*scratching*, **thud**/*scratching* on the hurriedly closing doors,
scoring the harsh truth of the Bosch's hell that we have made ourselves,
that we now must live

Doom   **Doom**   **Doom**   **Doom**   **Doom**
        !Scatter   *!Scatter*   *!Scatter*   *!Scatter*

Where?
Hills cannot hide us, whiplashed by roads into near-nakedness
the scars of houses lurid in the rents of landscape

Doom
        !Scatter

Where?
No place a battering ram bass guitar won't breach

Doom
        !Scatter

Where?

No burglar bar, security fence, no chain, no cord
a one-drop slashing hand cannot chop through

Doom
!Scatter

The downbeat beatdown dark tread sounding
deep into a stagnant too long ditch
a dread quaking, basal black reverberating doom, **doom**, **Doom**
cracking the clagged surfaces of tepid lives that spew apart and scatter

!Scatter   !Scatter . . .

But if, beyond this song, we listen —
what is it
that will — soon, soon — fall,
soon befall?
If we could squint up through the sludge that has become us,
if we could seer through the occluding scum, the self-colluding sly meniscus
cloying against the light searching our toxic depths,
if we could, through even one momentary mosaic crack of vision, see beyond —
what would it be, that brightening black dread
crescendoing from the cosmos down
to our end?

Doom   **Doom**   **Doom**   **Doom**   **Doom**
!Scatter   !Scatter   !Scatter   !Scatter

Listen, the beast
is telling us, the heart-shocking beat
of its drop-dragging, maimed feet, *it-a-come*, approaching louder
is the rough overture of a tough, defensively offensive,
off-beat deliberately always
          friend.

Doom
          !Scatter
                    Doom
                         !Scatter
                    Doom
                              !Scatter . . .
                                   !Scatter . . . !Scatter . . .

THREE ASPECTS OF THE NAME

Mark McMorris

I. The Stencil of My Device

At the threshold of morning I encountered a ghost, my name.
We quarreled, because I was of a more venerable caste
than what the name announced, a violent clan of laborers,
men given to dance in the costume of underworld spirits
who took ship with the merchants from the Gold Coast, and blew
ashore in the Latitudes of Weeping. Skilled at the machete
we cut down trees to fashion a secret bivouac in the hills.
The regiment came, flying the colors, to scatter and perish.
As time went on the news of these battles wore away
like earth from constant rainfall. We went from the hills
to settle the fertile lands about the capital. My ancestors
bore sons and daughters to men who reached the plantation
by other routes, and with other prospects. Hence the stencil
of my device, invisible to mirrors, but still vocal
like the echo of grief, which we alone perceive, detached
from the body though not replaced. The name remembers
events best left to the whistle of tree frogs at night.
A scent of orchids disguises the past, whereas the name
like a breeze in the pines infiltrates the landscape
and causes discomfort. Crickets whir in the midnight grass.

The gospel tells us that tradition flows like a river
to irrigate the soul, from origin to the fringe
of reason. It is the thing you can't avoid belonging to
just as the sea cannot escape mingling with water.
The voice of tradition is ours, or else we are empty
forms cast aside like husks from a coconut grove
able to lie in the sun but not to speak of the havoc
of hunger, or so the philosophers aver, in their moods.
The history of the tribe is fixed within the orbit
traced by the name in written records. Nothing else exists.

II. The Stream at Mavis Bank

The stream at Mavis Bank overflows the roadway.
The place is forever tinted in sunlight —
the water slipping around boulders, twisting
flows dipping and boiling over with froth.
To bathe in this stream is a rite of passage.
Deep or shallow, the water saturates the name
fetched from the city, together with the language
that cradles its previous owners, the planters
in high boots wading through guinea grass
toward a millhouse, stolid in the morning dew.

On the island, nothing is hidden; every surface
contains the whole of the pattern, like a fractal
shape reproducing an arabesque of error
sutured to integral gesture, the confident practice
of place. The river escapes from this pattern.
The water flows without warning, into the middle
of a road, to supplant the archival voice.
No scribe has planted the river into memory.
Cold water on the skin at dawn is the only naming.

III. The Dominion of Grammaticus

The river is always flowing, always there
it fills the stanza of the dithyramb
with forces and driftwood and cadence.
It unites here with the wild. It connects
seaport to inland sea to urban oasis
of unsuitable livery, worn at the sleeve.

＊

To believe that a name fits you badly
like a suit of creaky armor, or the name
turns prism into prison, and filters light
as interference pattern, surely it is
that this purpose is given in the nature
of signs, which drop from above. For the name
belongs to the dominion of Grammaticus.

＊

The epic narrative, rolling forward,
soon discovers an old man kneeling
to kiss the hands that took the life
of his son. That's what it says
plain as snowy Atlas and Olympus.
Camped by the sea, the alien tribe
is my force, my people. The scout leaning
at the cave door watches the road
to the mountain bivouac, where song
is forbidden. No epic tradition records
this passage to liberty of the dead.

For Colin Channer

Sing the Union cause, sing us / the poor, the marginal.
—Robert Hayden, "Homage to Paul Robeson"

Preamble

Note the confection of your body
salt on the breeze, the corn
silk sky. Olmstead's signature
archways and meadows. Kite
strings tensing the load of a saddle-
backed wind. This is Prospect Park,
Brooklyn, where limbs tickle
and jounce as if ice cubes shivered
along the shirtsleeves of evergreens. Pond
water whispers, and the echoes of Yankee
fifes linger in wind and in the shirring jazz
hands of leaves, and those shirts,
the skins, the human retinue converging
on the uneven playing fields. The African
drum and dance circle sways the pignut
tree into a charismatic trance as
Orthodox women walk powerfully by, jogging
shoes blinking beneath the billows of their
skirts, children rollerblading, trailing
tzitzits. Take heart in the percussion
structuring the distance like prophetic
weather, a shelter of vibrations:
the last conga note a bolt tapped into
the day's doorframe and you are no less,
no more home here than in the corridors
you return to in your dreams. Illusory,

altogether babel-fractured, a single word
from you might bring the verdant funhouse
down. Listen like a safecracker, navigate
the intricate ruptures by ear: the Latin
patois of picnickers, the Slavic tongues
of lovers replacing your mouth with self-
conscious silence. You are Caliban
and Crusoe, perpetual stranger with a fork
in the socket of life's livid grid,
stunned and bewildered at the frank
intrusion of the mosquito on the hairless
back of your hand. You are stranded
at the limit, extremity and restriction,
jealous for that elusive — the domestic, yes,
you're thinking: not the brick and mortar, but
the quickening backfill of belonging, the stranger-
facing, the neighbor-knowing confidence and ease
with the ripple that diminishes as it extends
over the vast potential of immovable thirst.
You are home now, outsider, for what that's worth.

Problemata

In the *Preamble*, Gouverneur Morris refers, poetically,
to the "domestic tranquility" shattered by rebelling
war veterans who, unable to pay mounting war taxes, confronted
the state for having seized their homes. The veterans argued
their point with bayonets fixed to their flintlock rifles. Point being
that blood should have been enough, as it was in their barter
economy, to square their debt in the Revolution.
Morris could not abide an economy that imagined exchange

in such finite terms. For him, every shilling appraised on an altar
of speculative devotions, every home subject to the metaphoric
notion of home, the value of tranquility proportionate
to the power one has to gerrymander that metaphor.

❋

Consider the dear evangelists who canvass our homes
Saturday mornings, who share their pamphlets and good
words, their domestic concerns swelling with their
longing for the fellowship of us. Spinoza gives us
this reason not to opt off of their call lists: *The good,*
which a man desires for himself and loves, he will love
more constantly, if he sees that others love it also;
he will therefore endeavor that others should love it also.
Be tolerant of their attention, their pursuit of agape
love a planet-sized chip they bear on their shoulders
from house to house, door to door,
blessing whatever they find inside.

❋

I recently friended my brother on a
social networking website.
It is possible we will never
have to speak again. Why speak
when we have a crystal ball
of software through which
to judge one another's lives?
I imagine this is what
the afterlife will be like.
I'm ghost, we say
instead of goodbye.

❋

It is nearly July in Brooklyn and already
the fireworks from Chinatown warehouses

193

are bursting in stellar fluorescence like tinsel-tied
dreadlocks above the Bushwick tenements and the brownstone
blocks of Bed-Stuy now littered with the skittering
decollage of wrappers exploded across blacktops and handball
courts, playgrounds and sidewalks knuckled by tree roots.
My neighbor's teenaged boys argued who possessed the greatest
patriotism. Just as pit bulls chained to their fists intend
to exemplify their precariously domesticated manhood,
they sought to demonstrate their patriotism with bottle
rockets, spinners, petards, these household paraphernalia of war.
The competition was vigorous, drew spectators and blood.
When the smoke cleared, no charges
were filed. We neighbors wavered distractedly a moment
before tracing our paths back into our quiet homes.

Problema 1

Because Venus lifted the Rosewater Dish like a shield
in the sun the graying father of two swatted a juggle
of balls against a playground wall that had been graffitied
for an episode of *Law & Order* set in the hood.
The desiccated catgut of his racket strummed
like a junkyard harp with each gouty ground stroke.
A muscle fire stoked to warm the bagpipes in his chest.
Like a waft of charcoal in the park, there came to him
thought of the bargain implied in God's command
to Abraham. Not unlike Robert Johnson's deal
at the crossroads or Gauguin's pricey escape from
the obscurity of the middle class, these appeals
to the brute motives of the blood,
mortal insecurity seeking relief in the barter

for fertility or fame. This was the mind of the man
as he stiffened and hid his wind in a falsely barreling
chest, setting out to retrieve what may have seemed
portentous —a citrine moon descending
on the shirtless men playing handball
on the opposite court, an intrusion like a cell phone
ringing in Alice Tully Hall. Their annoyance was muted
but palpable for they, too, were performing
the ritual of their devotions. What he wouldn't give to hear,
like a nest of hungering chicks, his flock, the epochal
cry of thousands in the stadium around Centre Court,
his name on the wind. Perhaps he'd swap it all for the boy
he once was, the future altered, and follow
some stellar herald, righteousness and treason
arcing in his mind like a halo, to risk a life
he could only begin to imagine.

Problema 2

> *My father, they have killed me!*
> —Chinua Achebe, *Things Fall Apart*

Consider throwing the baby from the window a figure
of speech barely reaching across the fence separating
expression from intent. *For all our sake,* I tell my wife,
I'm going to throw the baby out the window now,
as I rise from the sofa in response to the midnight
wail of another footie uprising heard among
the moans and whines of our neighbors' appliances
and the various alarms of the city's eternal self-soothing.
The ancient hardwood floor in the bedroom upstairs
groaning under thirty-pound footsteps for the fourth time

tonight. It is nearly July in Brooklyn. Windows are open.
Consider the neighbors grimacing, pillowing
their ears to shield against the little one's battle cry.

Because I am teaching Euripides in the fall, I am
reading him now between commercial breaks, and
imagining far-flung Brooklyn quorumed in the armories
and in streets beneath the ginkgoes and buttonwoods,
crowds gathered to mandate I quiet my lamb eternally.
What if my neighbors read my hyperbole as oath, made me
keep my word? Who would I betray? Would I smuggle
my mewling daughter to Canada, flee this land? I do love
Brooklyn so. I have lent a neighborly ear to elderly
West Indians on the B44 from Bed-Stuy to Flatbush.
Heard them lament Yankee reluctance to use
old-country discipline, which, they claim, is the only real
solution to this climate of "gang foolery." Spanking. Yes.
The sacramental rod tanning backsides of the elect few,
a ritual hazing to appease the divinity of the unknowable
and omnipresent urban populace. Consider the vanity
of sacrifice, the paper tiger of blind devotion fanning
the dander of a timid hand. Consider Agamemnon,
victim of pride and contagion, raising that hand
against his child at Aulis, the inexorable machinery of tribalism
grinding away the primacy of paternal love. Beware the prophet,
the genie, the divine stranger who, with a wink, unmasks your
arrogant self-images, who finds the harmonic note that gathers
your most discordant emotions toward the mute
accumulation of will. *What I do this night*
I do for you, Brooklyn, I offer,
as the banister whimpers beneath my trembling hand.

Problema 3

The Fulton St. Foodtown is playing Motown and I'm surprised
at how quickly my daughter picks up the tune. And soon
the two of us, plowing rows of goods steeped in fructose
under light thick as corn oil, are singing *Baby,*
I need your lovin, unconscious of the lyrics' foreboding.
My happy child riding high in the shopping cart as if she's
cruising the polished aisles in a Zamboni laden with imperishable
foodstuffs. Her cornball father enthusiastically prompting
with spins and flourishes and the double-barrel fingers
of the gunslinger's pose. But we hear it as we round the rice
and Goya aisle, that other music, the familiar exchange of anger,
the war drums of parent and child. The boy wants, what, to be
carried? to eat the snacks right from his mother's basket?
What does it matter, he is making a scene. With no self-interest
beyond the pleasure of replacing wonder with wonder, my daughter
asks me to name the boy's offense. I offer to buy her ice cream.
How can I admit recognizing the portrait of fear the mother's face
performs, the inherited terror of nonconformity frosted with the fear
of being thought disrespected by, or lacking the will to discipline
one's child? How can I account for both the cultural and the inter-
cultural? The boy's cries rising like hosannas as the mother's purse
falls from her shoulder. Her missed step from the ledge
of one of her stilted heels, passion loosed with each displaced
hairpin. His little jacket bunched at the collar where she has worked
the marionette. Later, when I'm placing groceries on the conveyor
belt and it is clear I've forgotten the ice cream, my daughter
tries her hand at this new algorithm of love, each word
punctuated by her little fist: *Boy,* she commands, *didn't I tell you?*

Problema 4

At thirteen I asked my father for a tattoo.
I might as well have asked for a bar mitzvah.
He said I had no right to alter the body
he gave me. Aping what little of Marx I learned
from the sisters down the street who wore torn
black stockings with Doc Martens and gave me
rides to school in their sticker-covered
hatchback, I said I was a man because I could claim
my body and the value of its labor. This meant
I could adorn it or dispose of it as I chose. Tattoos,
my father said, are like children: have one,
you'll want another. I knew there was a connection
between the decorated body and reproduction.
This is why I wanted a tattoo. Yet I reasoned,
not in so many words, his analogy only held
in the case of possession, i.e., I possess my body,
but cannot possess my children. His laughter
was my first lesson in the human Ponzi
scheme of paternalism, the self-electing
indenture to the promise of material inheritance,
men claiming a hollow authority simply
because their fathers had claimed
a hollow authority. Knowing I had little
idea as to what my proposed tattoo might
resemble, my father sent me to my room
to sketch it using the pastels he had given me
for Christmas. Based on his critique, he said,
he would consider my request. But he had
already taken the shine from my swagger.
How can I beautify what I do not possess

and call it anything but graffiti? Chris Rock says
my first job is to keep my daughter
off the pole. Although I have expended
great energy arguing the autonomy of strippers,
I have to agree with him. As a father myself
I now see every mutinous claim of independence
as the first steps toward my sweet pea's
falling in with a bad crowd. Richard Pryor
says we are bound to fuck up our kids
one way or another. My father would
split the difference: *I made you*, he'd say,
*I can unmake you, and make another one
just like you.*

#1

You should start talking about the half–Puerto Rican girl
in your workshop who used a palm tree in her symbol exercise.
Paradise, she says. *That's what it means.*
You tell her that on the way to workshop
your taxi caught a red light at the intersection
of Fernández Juncos y Avenida Kennedy in Santurce
& you saw Anacaona sitting under a palm tree,
picking shingles off her arms. You saw her
do a sloppy open back to outside turn toward your car
& break into a salsa rendition of Jingle Bells.
She pushed her beat-up, super-size Burger King cup
against the driver's window, asked for some epidemic chip-ins,
because her habit just got bigger by one trimester.
Freddy the Touristica driver said that you
don't see what you just saw in the tourist guides,
so *fíjate.*

#2

Real will recognize real once they see
that your your R's were traded for L's
& your S's got clipped somewhere
across the Atlantic.
Don't go to the beach in the winter —
you won't find real Puerto Ricans &
at least three construction workers
from DR will opine that if PR
goes free the sand will go quick &
you just ain't ready for that kind of noise.

#3

On the way to pick up his financial aid package,
Carlito received a voicemail from his Tío Pedro.
It said that Mami Juanita just walked into a precinct,
strapped head-to-toe with dynamite sticks,
demanding that the San Juan Ritz-Carlton Casino
give back all her Social Security checks.

#4

First Tuesday of every month
dale pa Viejo San Juan, Noches de Galería.
Beware of bleached trigueñas, dudes
who thread their eyebrows & pro-statehood politicos
who use bomba y plena groups to fundraise.
Tap a cobblestone for good luck and with
the best of luck you'll end up at Café Seda,
on your tenth can of Medalla, DJ Velcro
spinning the summer jam out of you.
You might even try to get symbolic with it
& puff a blunt by El Morro, putting yourself
in the persona of the first dude who saw Columbus
& told him to take off the brim, lose the doublet,
get rid of the girdle, it's hot, yo & you being
the Paseo Boricua that you are,
the dirt-eating Ponceña that you are,
the Filiberto Ojeda Ríos that you are,
the che-che-cole that you are, the thirty
seconds it takes to steal a car that you are,
the olive skin Buddhist pop star that you are,

will pass Columbus the blunt & tell him to
take a hit before the government is forced
to shut down for a day.

#5

Now remember — your conjugation game
needs to be tight. It's true — Puerto Ricans
love for free. But in the immortal words
of my compay John, "What the fuck is a *vosotros*?"
After the first ¡hola! you will be from out there,
de afuera, no matter your authentic Taíno DNA pattern,
no matter how many boleros Abuelo sang when you were born,
no matter how many flags are hanging out your window.
You don't hear as many coquís these days so when
the mic opens remember how Don Pedro blasted
the interrogator with that me cago en la madre
que te pario, cabron, but you have to make sure
that you do it all in lengua madre because there will be
that one dude dressed in full black regalia who will
crash your class, set fire to a stolen PNP poster &
without saying whaddup, what's going on brother,
he will ask you, the Visiting Nuyorican Poet,
if you know Spanish.

CHRIS ABANI's prose includes *Song for Night*, *The Virgin of Flames*, *Becoming Abigail*, and *GraceLand*. His poetry collections include *Hands Washing Water*, *Dog Woman*, *Daphne's Lot*, and *Kalakuta Republic*. He is a professor at the University of California, Riverside, and a recipient of the PEN/Barbara Goldsmith Freedom to Write Award, the Prince Claus Award, a Lannan Literary Fellowship, a California Book Award, a Hurston/Wright Legacy Award, a PEN/Beyond Margins Award, a Hemingway Foundation/PEN Award, and a Guggenheim Fellowship. For more information, visit www.chrisabani.com.

OPAL PALMER ADISA is the author of *I Name Me Name*, a collection of autobiographical prose, dramatic monologue, lyric poem, praise song, blues, and prophetic rant; and a new novel, *Painting Away Regrets*. Her previous books include *Until Judgment Comes*, *Bake-Face and Other Guava Stories*, *Eros Muse*, *It Begins with Tears*, *Caribbean Passion*, *Tamarind*, and *Mango Women*, winner of the PEN Oakland/ Josephine Miles Award. Born in Jamaica, Adisa teaches literature and creative writing, and is the former chair of the Ethnic Studies/Cultural Diversity program at the California College of Arts in Oakland. For more information, visit www.opalpalmeradisa.com.

ELIZABETH ALEXANDER is a poet, essayist, playwright, and teacher. She was born in New York City and raised in Washington, D.C. Her collections of poetry include *American Sublime*, a finalist for the Pulitzer Prize, *Antebellum Dream Book*, *Body of Life*, and *The Venus Hottentot*. She also coauthored, with Marilyn Nelson, *Miss Crandall's School for Young Ladies & Little Misses of Color*. She received the Jackson Poetry Prize from *Poets & Writers*, the Quantrell Award for Excellence in Undergraduate Teaching at the University of Chicago, and the George Kent Award, given by Gwendolyn Brooks. She has served as a faculty member for Cave Canem poetry workshops, and is currently the chair of the African American Studies Department at Yale University. She was selected to compose and read a poem, "Praise Song for the Day," at Barack Obama's presidential inauguration in 2009.

MEENA ALEXANDER was born in India and raised both there and in Sudan. She is distinguished professor of English at Hunter College and the Graduate Center at the City University of New York. She has published numerous poetry collections, including *Illiterate Heart*, which won the PEN/Beyond Margins Award, *Raw Silk*, and *Quickly Changing River*. She is also the author of an autobiography, *Fault Lines*, chosen as one of *Publishers Weekly*'s Best Books of 1993; two novels, *Nampally Road* and *Manhattan Music*; a book of poems and essays, *The Shock of Arrival: Reflections on Postcolonial Experience*; and two academic studies, one of which is *Women in Romanticism: Mary Wollstonecraft, Dorothy Wordsworth, and Mary Shelley*.

NICHOLAS ALEXANDER was born on January 7, 1976, in Kingston, Jamaica. He received his bachelor's degree in English and philosophy, and his master's in religious and ethical studies. His poems have been published in *Caribbean Voice*, along with the *Jamaica Observer* and the *Jamaica Gleaner*. In 2008 he became a fellow of the Calabash International Literary Festival Writer's Workshop.

GABEBA BADEROON is a South African author of three collections of poetry, *The Dream in the Next Body*, *The Museum of Ordinary Life*, and *A Hundred Silences*. *The Dream in the Next Body* was a Notable Book of 2005 in the *Sunday Independent* in South Africa, and *A Hundred Silences* was a Writer's Choice Book of 2006 in the *Independent* in Nigeria. Baderoon received a Guest Writer's Grant at the Nordic Africa Institute, and a Civitella Ranieri Fellowship. She is also the recipient of the 2005 DaimlerChrysler Award for South African poetry. For more information, visit www.gabeba.com.

AMIRI BARAKA was born Everett LeRoi Jones in 1934 in Newark, New Jersey. His numerous literary honors include fellowships from the Guggenheim Foundation and the National Endowment for the Arts, the PEN/Faulkner Award, the Rockefeller Foundation Award for Drama, the Langston Hughes Award from the City College of New York, and a lifetime achievement award from the Before Columbus Foundation. He was inducted into the American Academy of Arts and Letters in 1995, and in 2002 was named Poet Laureate of New Jersey and Newark Public Schools. His book of short stories, *Tales of the Out & the Gone*, was published in late 2007 to great critical acclaim by Akashic Books. Two of his groundbreaking essay collections from the 1960s, *Home* and *Black Music*, have also recently been reissued by Akashic. For more information, visit www.amiribarakabooks.com.

EDWARD BAUGH is emeritus professor of English at the University of the West Indies, Mona. He was born in the town of Port Antonio, Jamaica, and educated at Titchfield School, the University College of the West Indies, Queen's University in Ontario, Canada, and the University of Manchester. His book *Derek Walcott*, a critical study, was published in 2006, and he has also written two collections of poetry, *A Tale from the Rainforest* and *It Was the Singing*.

CHARLIE BOBUS, a.k.a. Nicardo Murray, writes a new genre of poetry called motivational dub poetry. He is an activist, producer, publisher, event promoter/coordinator, actor, workshop facilitator, and motivational speaker. With extensive experience on stage shows, festivals, and the live poetry circuit, he has toured Canada, Trinidad, and Barbados. He is the author of the book *Creative Energy*.

ROGER BONAIR-AGARD, a Cave Canem fellow, is a native of Trinidad and Tobago. He is the author of two collections of poetry, *Tarnish and Masquerade* and *GULLY*, and is a coauthor of *Burning Down the House*. A two-time National Poetry Slam champion, he is the cofounder and artistic director of the LouderARTS Project, a poet-in-residence with the interdisciplinary ensemble VisionIntoArt, a recipient of a Vox Ferus writer's residency, and also writes and performs the critically acclaimed one-man show *Masquerade: Calypso and Home*. Bonair-Agard splits his time between Brooklyn and Chicago.

CHERYL BOYCE-TAYLOR, Trinidad-born and Queens-bred, is a poet, as well as a visual and teaching artist. The author of three collections of poetry, *Raw Air*, *Night When Moon Follows*, and *Convincing the Body*, and a recipient of the Partners in Writing Grant, Boyce-Taylor served as Poet in Residence at the Caribbean Literary and Cultural Center in Brooklyn. Her poems have been anthologized in various publications including *Pank*, *Naugatuck River Review*, *Def Poetry Jam's Bum Rush the*

Page, Poetry Nation, Carry the Word, and *ALOUD: Voices from the Nuyorican Poets Café*. Boyce-Taylor holds master's degrees in both education and social work, and graduated from the Stonecoast MFA in Creative Writing program at the University of Southern Maine. For more information, visit www.cherylboycetaylor.com.

DIONNE BRAND is a poet, novelist, and essayist living in Toronto. Her nine volumes of poetry include *Land to Light On*, which won the Governor General's Award for Poetry and the Trillium Book Award. Brand's most recent volume of verse, *Inventory*, was nominated for the Governor General's Award. Her latest novel, *What We All Long For*, was published to great acclaim in Canada, Italy, and Germany. Her fiction includes the collection *Sans Souci and Other Stories* and *In Another Place Not Here*, a 1998 *New York Times* Notable Book. Her works of nonfiction include *Bread Out of Stone*, a book of essays, and *A Map to the Door of No Return*, a meditation on blackness in the Diaspora.

JEAN "BINTA" BREEZE, an actress and poet, grew up in rural Jamaica before moving to Kingston, where she soon established herself as a writer, performer, and recording artist. Often backed with the rhythms and reverberations of reggae, Breeze is known primarily as a dub poet and recorded the album *Tracks* with the Dennis Bovell Dub Band. She studied at what was then the Jamaica School of Drama, now the Edna Manley College of the Visual and Performing Arts. Her publications include *On the Edge of an Island*, a collection of poetry and prose, *Ryddim Ravings*, which was also released as an album, and *Spring Cleaning*. Her fifth and most recent book of poems, *The Fifth Figure*, was published in 2006.

SIMON PHILLIP BROWN was born in Kingston, Jamaica, and graduated from Ohio Wesleyan University in 2008 with a bachelor of arts in creative writing and a minor in black world studies. His poems have been published in the *Jamaica Observer*, Ohio Wesleyan's literary magazine, the *OWL*, and the *African Weekender* of Ohio. He has since returned to Jamaica and is currently a teacher, coach, poet, and rapper. He received a fellowship for the Calabash Writer's Workshop in 2008.

LENWORTH BURKE is a fellow of the Wayne Brown Writers' Workshop and the Cropper Foundation of Trinidad and Tobago. Primarily a writer of fiction, his short stories and poems have been published in a number of newspapers and anthologies. He is an attorney in private practice.

CHRISTIAN CAMPBELL is a poet, academic, and culture worker of Bahamian and Trinidadian heritage. He studied at Oxford as a Rhodes Scholar and received a PhD at Duke. He is the author of *Running the Dusk* and currently teaches at the University of Toronto.

COLIN CHANNER is the founder and artistic director of the Calabash International Literary Festival Trust. He was born in Jamaica, but has lived in the U.S. since his late teens. Known primarily as a novelist, he is the Newhouse Visiting Professor in Creative Writing at Wellesley College near Boston, Massachusetts.

STACEYANN CHIN was one of the original performers and cowriters of *Russell Simmons Def Poetry Jam* on Broadway, which won a Tony Award in 2004. She was also featured on the five seasons of the Peabody Award–winning HBO series *Def Poetry Jam*. Born in Jamaica, Chin lives in Brooklyn, New York. Her poems can be found in numerous anthologies and in her chapbooks: *Wildcat Woman, Stories Surrounding My Coming, Catalogue the Insanity,* and *Mad Hatter*. Under the umbrella of the Culture Project, she has written and performed three one-woman shows: *Hands Afire, Unspeakable Things,* and *Border/Clash*. Author of the memoir *The Other Side of Paradise,* Chin has been awarded the Carnegie Transformation Residency as an Equity Scholar at the University of Witwatersrand in Johannesburg, South Africa. For more information, visit www.staceyannchin.com.

GEORGE ELLIOTT CLARKE was born in Three Mile Plains, Nova Scotia. A celebrated African Canadian poet, novelist, playwright, opera librettist, and scholar, he is currently a professor of English at the University of Toronto. His noted books include *Whylah Falls,* winner of the Archibald Lampman Award; *Execution Poems,* recipient of the Governor General's Award for Poetry; *George & Rue,* winner of the Dartmouth Book Award for Fiction; and *Blues and Bliss: The Poetry of George Elliott Clarke,* recipient of the Eric Hoffer Book Award. His 2009 book, *I & I,* is a verse novel about a couple traveling from Nova Scotia to Texas and encountering tragedies of racism and sexism.

MEL COOKE wrote his first poem as an adult, "This Is Jamaica," in 1996, and didn't read it publicly until 2000. Writing mainly intuitively, his first exposure to formal poetry was through the 2007/2008 Calabash Writer's Workshop. His debut collection, *11/9,* was published in 2008.

NATALIE G.S. CORTHÉSY's work has been published in the *Daily Gleaner* and the *Carimac Times*. She is the recipient of many awards in the Jamaica Cultural Development Commission's National Festival of the Arts Creative Writing Competition, including two silver medals, two bronze medals, and several merits. She is currently working on her first collection of poems.

MARSHA-JAY DALLAS's poetry reflects a minimalist approach that combines personal and abstract elements. Several of her poems have been published in the *Jamaica Observer* and the *Jamaica Gleaner*. She is a graduate student at the University of the West Indies and is working on her first collection of poetry.

KWAME DAWES was born in Ghana and raised in Jamaica. He is the author of fourteen books of poetry and many books of fiction, nonfiction, criticism, and drama; and editor of several anthologies of poetry. His debut novel, *She's Gone,* published by Akashic Books, was a finalist for the Hurston/Wright Legacy Award. He is Distinguished Poet in Residence at the University of South Carolina where he directs the SC Poetry Initiative and the school's Arts Institute, and is the programming director of the Calabash International Literary Festival.

TOI DERRICOTTE was born in Hamtramck, Michigan, in 1941. Her books of poetry are *Tender,* winner of the 1998 Paterson Poetry Prize, *Captivity, Natural Birth,* and *The Empress of the Death House*. *The Black Notebooks,* a literary memoir, won the 1998 Anisfield-Wolf Book Award for Nonfiction and was a *New York Times* Notable Book of the Year. Her essay, "Beginning Dialogues," is included in the *Best American Essays*

2006, edited by Lauren Slater. Her honors include the Lucille Medwick Memorial Award from the Poetry Society of America; two Pushcart Prizes; the Distinguished Pioneering of the Arts Award from the United Black Artists; and fellowships from the National Endowment for the Arts, the New Jersey State Council on the Arts, the Rockefeller Foundation, the Guggenheim Foundation, and the Maryland State Arts Council. With Cornelius Eady, in 1996, she cofounded Cave Canem Foundation, North America's premier home for black poetry. She is a professor of English at the University of Pittsburgh. For more information, visit www.toiderricotte.com.

RICHARD "DINGO" DINGWALL started writing in 1994 and joined the Jamaica Poetry Society in 1995. He recorded the album *Ransom* in 2000, a delicate blend of music and poetry; a video for the song "Earth Speaks" was voted Video of the Year by the Caribbean Broadcasting Union. A winner of the Caribbean Music Expo Talent Search in 2001, Dingo has been featured at the Calabash Literary Festival, Reggae Sumfest with the Zinc Fence Band, and at Reggae Sunsplash 2006. He started the edgy T-shirt line Hardmore Gear in 2005 and is currently working on material for a second album.

CORNELIUS EADY, a Cave Canem cofounder, was born in Rochester, New York. He is the author of *Brutal Imagination* (a National Book Award finalist), *Autobiography of a Jukebox, You Don't Miss Your Water, The Gathering of My Name*, and *Victims of the Latest Dance Craze*, which was the Lamont Poetry Selection of the Academy of American Poets. His honors include the Prairie Schooner Strousse Award and fellowships from the Guggenheim Foundation, the National Endowment for the Arts, the Rockefeller Foundation, and the Lila Wallace-*Reader's Digest* Foundation. His collaboration with jazz composer Deidre Murray has resulted in several musical theater works, including *You Don't Miss Your Water, Running Man* (a finalist for the Pulitzer Prize), *Fangs*, and *Brutal Imagination*. He is presently associate professor of English at the University of Notre Dame.

BLAKKA ELLIS is a writer, teacher, and performing artist. He studied at the Jamaica School of Drama, the University of the West Indies, and York University. He cowrote the national pantomime *Schoolers*, which won the Jamaica Music Industry Award for Best Musical in 1989; *Laugh Jamaica*, which won the Actor Boy Award for Best Revue 1998; and wrote, directed, and starred in *Tings a Gwaan: The Comedy Revue*—voted Best Comedy and nominated for Best New Jamaican Play in the 2004 Actor Boy Awards. Ellis also writes a weekly column in the Jamaican *Star* newspaper. A Calabash Writer's Workshop Fellow, his poetry chapbook *Gateman* was published in 2005.

TOMLIN ELLIS was born in St. Catherine, Jamaica, in 1955. He is a founding member of the groups Poets in Unity and the Poetry Society of Jamaica. One of the early participants of the Calabash Writer's Workshops and a performer at the first Calabash Festival in 2001, Ellis also represented Jamaica at the ninth annual Poetry Festival held in Medellín, Colombia. A media practitioner and trainer with over thirty years of experience in the broadcast industry, he produced one of Jamaica's longest-running radio poetry programs, *Groundings*, which aired on JBC Radio in the 1970s and featured Miss Lou, Mervyn Morris, Edward Baugh, Lorna Goodison, and many others.

MARTÍN ESPADA was born in Brooklyn, New York, in 1957. He has published sixteen books as a poet, editor, and translator. His eighth book of poems, *The Republic of Poetry*, was a finalist for the Pulitzer Prize. His previous collection, *Alabanza: New and Selected Poems* (1982–2002), received the Paterson Award for Sustained Literary Achievement and was named an American Library Association Notable Book of the Year. An earlier collection, *Imagine the Angels of Bread*, won an American Book Award and was a finalist for the National Book Critics Circle Award. He has received numerous other honors, including the Robert Creeley Award, the Antonia Pantoja Award, an Independent Publisher Book Award, a Gustavus Myers Outstanding Book Award, the Paterson Poetry Prize, the Charity Randall Citation, the PEN/Revson Fellowship, a Guggenheim Foundation Fellowship, and two NEA Fellowships. A former tenant lawyer, Espada is a professor in the Department of English at the University of Massachusetts, Amherst, where he teaches creative writing and the work of Pablo Neruda. For more information, visit www.martinespada.net.

MAKESHA EVANS has been writing poems, songs, and short stories since the age of seven. A recipient of a fellowship with the Calabash International Literary Festival Trust, Evans is a psychologist and acting principal of the Institute for Theological and Leadership Development, one of the constituent colleges of the International University of the Caribbean.

BERNARDINE EVARISTO was born and raised in London, where she currently lives. Her books include *Hello Mum*, a novella about teenage knife crime in Britain; *Lara*, a verse novel based on her family history spanning England, Nigeria, Ireland, Germany, and Brazil; *Blonde Roots*, a prose novel in which Africans enslave Europeans; *Soul Tourists*, a verse novel, which explores Europe's black history; *The Emperor's Babe*, a verse novel about a black girl growing up in Roman London nearly 2000 years ago. Her awards include the Orange Prize Youth Panel Award, Arts Council Writer's Award, Big Red Read Award, EMMA Best Book Award, and a NESTA Fellowship Award. She was elected a fellow of the Royal Society of Literature in 2004, a fellow of the Royal Society of Arts in 2006, and was awarded an MBE in the Queen's Birthday Honours List in 2009. For more information, visit www.bevaristo.net.

NIKKY FINNEY was born in Conway, South Carolina, in 1957. A professor of creative writing at the University of Kentucky and a Cave Canem faculty member, Finney is the author of three books of poetry, *On Wings Made of Gauze*, *The World Is Round*, and *Rice*, which won a 1999 PEN America Open Book Award. She is also the author of *Heartwood*, a collection of short stories written especially for literacy students.

RUTH FORMAN, who won the Barnard New Women Poets Prize and appeared in the PBS series *The United States of Poetry*, is the author three poetry collections, *We Are the Young Magicians*, *Renaissance*, and *Prayers Like Shoes*; and a children's book, *Young Cornrows Callin Out the Moon*.

DELORES GAUNTLETT was born in St. Ann, Jamaica, in 1949. She is the author of *Freeing Her Hands to Clap* and *The Watertank Revisited*. Her poetry has appeared in the *Caribbean Writer*, *Poetry News*, *Kunapipi*, *Observer Literary Arts*, *Jamaica Journal*, *Calabash Journal*, *Sunday Gleaner*, *New Caribbean Poetry*, *Journal of Caribbean*

Literatures, among many others. Short-listed for the 2007 Hamish Canham Prize, her awards for poetry include the 1999 David Hough Prize and the 2006 *Daily News* Prize.

ARACELIS GIRMAY writes poetry, fiction, and essays. Her book of poems, *Teeth*, was a finalist for the Connecticut Book Award and won the GLCA New Writers Award. A graduate of Connecticut College and New York University, she is the recipient of grants from the Watson Foundation and the Jerome Foundation. She facilitates community writing workshops and she teaches at Drew University.

SUSAN GOFFE was born in Kingston, Jamaica, in 1957. A teacher of English who has been out of the formal system for many years, she is a Calabash Writer's Workshop Fellow.

LORNA GOODISON was born in Jamaica, and has received much recognition and many awards for her writing in both poetry and prose, including the Commonwealth Poetry Prize and Jamaica's Musgrave Gold Medal. She has published two collections of short stories, *Baby Mother and the King of Swords* and *Fool-Fool Rose Is Leaving Labour-in-Vain Savannah*. Her books of poetry include *Tamarind Season*, *I Am Becoming My Mother*, *Heartsease*, and *Controlling the Silver*. She teaches in the Department of English and the Center for Afro American and African Studies at the University of Michigan.

SAMUEL J. GORDON of Kingston, Jamaica, is a twenty-six-year-old writer, educator, and media practitioner. To date he is the youngest poet to represent the Poetry Society of Jamaica at the Calabash International Literary Festival.

MILLICENT GRAHAM was born in Kingston, Jamaica, in 1974. A Calabash Writer's Workshop Fellow, her first book of poems, *The Damp in Things*, was published in 2009.

SUHEIR HAMMAD is the author of *Born Palestinian Born Black*, *Drops of This Story*, *Zaatar Diva*, and, most recently, *breaking poems*. She was an original writer and performer for the Tony Award–winning *Russell Simmons Def Poetry Jam* on Broadway.

GHENET HARVEY has a BA in English and Spanish from Wesleyan College in Macon, Georgia, and an MA in Applied Translation Studies from London Metropolitan University in England. She lives and works in Jamaica as a copywriter.

SABRINA HAYEEM-LADANI, a native New Yorker, has performed her work across the United States for more than twelve years. She has been a featured poet at various venues including the Nuyorican Poets Café, Joe's Pub, Bar 13, Cornelia Street Café, and the Bowery Poetry Club. She studied theater and has trained as a flamenco dancer throughout Spain, and worked as a teaching artist in both New Mexico and New York City. Her poems have been published in the anthology *PARSE*, and she has self-published two collections: *Harsh Miracles* and *The Bone, The Weight*.

TERRANCE HAYES is the author of *Lighthead*, *Wind in a Box*, *Hip Logic*, and *Muscular Music*. His honors include a Whiting Writers Award, a National Endowment for the Arts Fellowship, and a Guggenheim Fellowship. A South Carolina native, he is a professor of creative writing at Carnegie Mellon University and lives in Pittsburgh, Pennsylvania, with his family.

JUSTINE HENZELL, a freelance producer, is the production director and one of the founders of the Calabash International Literary Festival. Born in Kingston, Jamaica, where she still resides, she oversees the legacy of *The Harder They Come*, the award-winning movie cowritten, produced, and directed by her father, Perry Henzell, which continues to reach a global audience over thirty years after its release.

SALLY HENZELL, an artist, poet, designer, and adventurer, lives and works in Treasure Beach, Jamaica, where she created the world-renowned boutique hotel, Jake's.

KENDEL HIPPOLYTE, born in St. Lucia in 1952, has published five books of poetry, the latest being *Night Vision,* and his work has appeared in various journals and anthologies. An award-winning playwright and theater director, he has received a James Michener Fellowship to study poetry, an OAS scholarship to study theater, and was awarded the St. Lucia Medal of Merit (Gold) in 2000 for his contribution to the arts.

ISHION HUTCHINSON was born in Port Antonio, Jamaica. He attended the University of the West Indies, Mona, and received his MFA from New York University. His work has appeared in the *LA Review, Callaloo,* and *Caribbean Review of Books.* He is a Calabash Writer's Workshop Fellow, and his first collection, *Far District,* will be published in 2010.

JOAN ANDREA HUTCHINSON is a writer, storyteller, actress, motivational speaker, and teacher. She is also a producer and presenter for radio and TV. She has been writing poems and stories in the Jamaican language for more than ten years, including *Meck Mi Tell Yuh,* a recent book of poems.

JONI JACKSON graduated from the University of the West Indies with a BS in geology, and currently lives and works in Kingston, Jamaica. She was a recipient of a Calabash Writer's Workshop Fellowship in 2006.

LINDA SUSAN JACKSON's first book of poetry, *What Yellow Sounds Like,* was a finalist for the Paterson Poetry Prize and the National Poetry Series Competition. She is also the author of two chapbooks, *Vitelline Blues* and *A History of Beauty,* and has received fellowships from the New York Foundation for the Arts, Frost Place, Soul Mountain Writers Retreat, Calabash, and Cave Canem. Her work has appeared in numerous anthologies and journals including *Ringing Ear: Black Poets Lean South, Gathering Ground, Crab Orchard Review, Rivendell, Brilliant Corners: A Journal of Jazz & Literature,* and *Heliotrope.* She is an associate professor of English at Medgar Evers College, City University of New York, in Brooklyn.

LINTON KWESI JOHNSON became only the second living poet and the first black poet, in 1982, to have his work included in Penguin's Modern Classics series. Born in the town of Chapelton, Jamaica, in 1952, he migrated to London in 1963; there, he attended Tulse Hill secondary school and later studied sociology at Goldsmiths

College, University of London. His books include *Inglan Is a Bitch* and, most recently, *Selected Poems*. Johnson's first album, *Dread Beat an' Blood*, was released in 1978. Since then he has released fourteen more, including *LKJ: Live in Paris* in 2004, a CD and DVD celebrating his twenty-fifth anniversary as a reggae recording artist. Johnson has been running his own record label, LKJ Records, since 1981. He has worked in journalism and still regularly tours around the world with the Dennis Bovell Dub Band.

NIKI JOHNSON's collection *skywalking* won a special commendation in the 1997 NBDC/NCB Awards. Her work has been published in the *Jamaica Observer* and *Calabash: A Journal of Caribbean Arts and Letters*. She has performed at the Poetry Society's monthly fellowship, taught at the Philip Sherlock Centre for the Creative Arts, and served as chief judge in the category of poetry for the Jamaica Cultural Development Commission. She was one of fifteen writers who performed at the 2000 World Expo in Hanover, Germany, for the Anna Blume Project in celebration of the artist/poet Kurt Schwitters. Her first collection *Weights and Measures* was published in the 2005 Calabash chapbook series.

JACKIE KAY, an adopted child of Scottish/Nigerian descent brought up by white parents in Glasgow, is one of Britain's best-known poets, appearing frequently on radio and TV programs about poetry and culture. Her most recent book, *Darling: New & Selected Poems*, combines many favorite poems from her four previous collections with new work. Her works of fiction include the novel *Trumpet* and two collections of short stories—*Why Don't You Stop Talking* and *Wish I Was Here*. Her honors include the Somerset Maugham Award, the *Guardian* Fiction Prize, and the Signal Poetry Award. She lives in Manchester, England.

YUSEF KOMUNYAKAA was born in Bogalusa, Louisiana, in 1947. His books of poems include: *Gilgamesh* (a verse play), *Pleasure Dome: New and Collected Poems, (1975–1999)*, *Talking Dirty to the Gods*, *Thieves of Paradise*, which was a finalist for the National Book Critics Circle Award, *Neon Vernacular: New and Selected Poems (1977–1989)*, which won the Pulitzer Prize and the Kingsley Tufts Poetry Award, *Magic City*, and *Dien Cai Dau*. His latest book, *Warhorses*, was published in 2008. Komunyakaa is currently a professor and Distinguished Senior Poet at New York University.

LI-YOUNG LEE's most recent book of poetry is *Book of My Nights*. His earlier works are *Rose*, winner of the Delmore Schwartz Memorial Award from New York University, *The City in Which I Love You*, a 1990 Lamont Poetry Selection; and a memoir entitled *The Winged Seed: A Remembrance*, which received an American Book Award from the Before Columbus Foundation. Lee's honors include fellowships from the National Endowment for the Arts, the Lannan Foundation, and the Guggenheim Foundation, as well as grants from the Illinois Arts Council, the Commonwealth of Pennsylvania, and the Pennsylvania Council on the Arts. In 1988, he received the Writer's Award from the Mrs. Giles Whiting Foundation. He lives in Chicago, Illinois, with his wife, Donna, and their two sons. Lee was born in 1957 in Jakarta, Indonesia, of Chinese parents.

ANN-MARGARET LIM, a fellow of the Calabash Writer's Workshop, has also participated in both the Mervyn Morris and Wayne Brown workshops. She has been published in the *Caribbean Writer*, *Caribbean Quarterly*, the *Journal of Caribbean Literature*, the *Pittsburgh Quarterly*, and *Calabash: A Journal of Caribbean Literature*. In 2007, she received a highly recommended designation for a poetry manuscript from the National Book Development Council of Jamaica.

RAYMOND MAIR was born in Jamaica in 1935. His poems have appeared in a number of publications, including the *Public Opinion Christmas Annual*, the *Sunday Observer*, the *Sunday Gleaner*, the *Caribbean Writer*, and *Calabash: A Journal of Caribbean Literature*; and in the anthologies *Focus*, *Bearing Witness 2 & 3*, and *Caribbean Poem*. He has received the Jamaica Festival Award and the *Observer* Literary Award.

devorah major became the third Poet Laureate of San Francisco in 2002. Her poetry books include *street smarts* and *where river meets ocean*. She is the author of two novels, *An Open Weave* and *Brown Glass Windows*, and has published poems, short stories, and essays in a number of magazines and anthologies. She has taught poetry and creative writing as a community artist in residence and college lecturer for over twenty years.

RACHEL MANLEY, daughter of the former Jamaican Prime Minister Michael Manley, was born in Cornwall, England, in 1947. At the age of two she was sent to Jamaica and was thereafter brought up by her grandparents, Norman and Edna Manley. Her first memoir *Drumblair: Memories of a Jamaican Childhood* was about those years and won the Canadian Governor General's Literary Award in 1997. She has since written two additional memoirs: *Slipstream: A Daughter Remembers*, about her father's political life and his final battle with cancer; and, most recently, *Horses in Her Hair: A Granddaughter's Story*, which tells the remarkable story of Edna Manley, who many regard as the mother of Jamaican art. Rachel Manley is currently working on another book, *The Applestrudle Tree*, and teaches creative writing at Lesley University in Cambridge, Massachusetts.

LORNE MATTHEWS was born in Kingston, Jamaica, in 1984. He attended Kingston College and the University of the West Indies, where he earned a BS in molecular biology. In recent years, he has written poetry, essays, and reviews, and has been published in the *Sunday Gleaner* and the *Jamaica Observer*. He is a Calabash Writer's Workshop Fellow.

MBALA's artistic journey began with the Self Theatrical Movement in Spanish Town, Jamaica, continuing at the Edna Manley College for the Visual and Performing Arts, and in drama groups such as Sistren Theatre Collective, where he was a set and costume designer, graphic artist, and musician. He is a member of Akwaaba de Drummers, the acoustic quartet Naseberry Jazz, and, with flutist/saxophonist Hugh "Papi" Pape, the Papiumba Big Band—which, despite its name, is a duo. Mbala's work has been published in several anthologies including *Focus 83*, *Wheel and Come Again: An Anthology of Reggae Poetry*, and *Voiceprint*. He is a vice president of the Poetry Society of Jamaica, and his first collection of poetry, *Light in a Book of Stone*, was published in the 2005 Calabash chapbook series.

EARL McKENZIE, born in St. Andrew, Jamaica, in 1943, was awarded a Silver Musgrave Medal in 2001 for his contribution to literature. He is the author of two collections of short stories, *A Boy Named Ossie* and *Two Roads to Mount Joyful*, and three collections of poetry, *Against Linearity*, *A Poet's House*, and *The Almond Leaf*, as well as one academic text, *Philosophy in the West Indian Novel*. McKenzie obtained his BA and MFA degrees from Columbia University, and his PhD from the University of British Columbia. He is a retired professor of philosophy.

MARK McMORRIS was born in Kingston, Jamaica, and attended the Excelsior School. He earned a bachelor's degree from Columbia University, and has a master's degree in creating writing (poetry) and a doctorate in comparative literature from Brown University. McMorris currently teaches at Georgetown University, and is the former director of its Lannan Center for Poetics and Social Practice. A two-time winner of the Contemporary Poetry Series Award from the University of Georgia Press, McMorris is the author of four books of poetry: *The Café at Light*, *The Blaze of the Poui*, *The Black Reeds*, and *Moth-Wings*.

NETO MEEKS is a member of the Poetry Society of Jamaica.

KEI MILLER was born in Jamaica in 1978. He has been a Vera Rubin Fellow at the Yaddo Arts Colony in New York and an International Writing Fellow at the University of Iowa. His books of poetry are *Kingdom of Empty Bellies* and *There Is an Anger that Moves*. His books of fiction include the short story collection *The Fear of Stones*, which was short-listed for a regional Commonwealth Writers' Prize, and a new novel, *The Same Earth*. Miller currently teaches creative writing at the University of Glasgow.

MERVYN MORRIS, born in Jamaica in 1937, studied at the University College of the West Indies and as a Rhodes Scholar at St. Edmund Hall, Oxford; he was a British Council Visiting Writer-in-Residence at the South Bank Centre in 1992. Morris lives in Kingston, Jamaica, where he is professor emeritus of creative writing and West Indian literature at the University of the West Indies. His poetry collections include *The Pond*, *Shadowboxing*, *Examination Centre*, *On Holy Week*, and *I been there, sort of: New & Selected Poems*. His critical work is included in *Making West Indian Literature* and *Is English We Speaking and Other Essays*. He has edited a number of books, including *It a Come* by Mikey Smith, *Selected Poems* by Louise Bennett, and *The Faber Book of Contemporary Caribbean Short Stories*.

VALZHYNA MORT, born in Minsk, Belarus, made her American debut in 2008 with the poetry collection *Factory of Tears*. She received the Crystal Vilenica Award in Slovenia in 2004, and won the Hubert Burda Prize for Eastern European poets in Germany in 2008. She is currently a writer in residence at the University of Baltimore.

HARRYETTE MULLEN was born in Alabama and grew up in Texas. Her books include *Tree Tall Woman*, *Trimmings*, *S*PeRM**K*T*, and *Muse & Drudge*—the latter three of which were collected into her most recent book, *Recyclopedia*, which received a PEN/Beyond Margins Award. In 2002, she published both *Blues Baby: Early Poems* and *Sleeping with the Dictionary*, a finalist for the National Book Award, the National Book Critics Circle Award, and the *Los Angeles Times* Book Prize in poetry. Mullen was the 2009 recipient of the Academy of American Poets Fellowship. Her other honors include artist grants from the Texas Institute of Letters and the Helene Wurlitzer Foundation of New Mexico, the Gertrude Stein Award in Innovative

American Poetry, and a Rockefeller Fellowship from the Susan B. Anthony Institute for Women's Studies at the University of Rochester. She teaches African American literature and creative writing in the English Department at the University of California, Los Angeles.

MUTABARUKA, born Allan Hope in 1952, is perhaps Jamaica's most famous living poet. He is also a recording artist and host of the *Cutting Edge*, a talk show on Irie FM. His collections of poetry include *Outcry, Sun and Moon*, and *The Book: First Poems*. He emerged on the music scene in 1981 with the release of the single "Every Time a Ear de Soun." Alligator Records released *Check It!*, his first of many albums, in 1983.

CHERRY NATURAL is a reggae poet whose work is influenced heavily by the everyday experiences of Jamaicans, and the sounds, rhythms, and creativity of generations of musicians and storytellers on the island. She began performing in 1979 and has toured the world with her poetry since then; she is also a motivational speaker, producer, and martial arts instructor with a black belt in Modern Arnis. She has published two collections of poetry, released a variety of spoken word recordings, and received numerous awards for her work.

MARILYN NELSON is a former Poet Laureate of the State of Connecticut. A three-time finalist for the National Book Award, and the holder of a Guggenheim Fellowship and two fellowships from the National Endowment for the Arts, Nelson is a graduate of the University of California, Davis, and holds postgraduate degrees from the University of Pennsylvania (MA) and the University of Minnesota (PhD). Her books include *For the Body, Mama's Promises, The Homeplace, Magnificat, The Fields of Praise: New and Selected Poems*, and *Carver: A Life in Poems*. Her rendition of Euripides' play, *Hecuba*, appears in *Euripides I*, the first volume of the Penn Greek Drama Series.

MICHAEL ONDAATJE is one of the world's foremost writers—his artistry and aesthetic have influenced an entire generation of writers and readers. Although he is best known as a novelist, Ondaatje's work also encompasses memoir, poetry, and film, and reveals a passion for defying conventional form. In his transcendent novel *The English Patient*—later made into the Academy Award–winning film—he explores the stories of people history fails to reveal, intersecting four diverse lives at the end of World War II. Ondaatje is himself an interesting intersection of cultures: Born in Sri Lanka, the former Ceylon, of Indian/Dutch ancestry, he went to school in England and then moved to Canada. He is now a Canadian citizen. From the memoir of his childhood, *Running in the Family*, to his Governor General's Award–winning book of poetry, *There's a Trick with a Knife I'm Learning to Do*, to his classic novel, *The English Patient*, Michael Ondaatje casts a spell over his readers. Having won the British Commonwealth's highest honor, the Booker Prize, he has taken his rightful place as a contemporary literary treasure.

OKU ONUORA, described by *Sounds* as "the original dub bard" and the "most disturbing performer of his genre," is a charismatic and passionate articulator of the grief and outrage of humanity's poor. He is widely credited with being the first artist to record dub poetry in Jamaica, and is respected around the world as an artistic and spiritual elder of this young but influential form. Onuora gained notoriety in Jamaica in the 1970s when he escaped prison twice after being arrested for armed robbery. While serving his sentence, Onuora wrote the play *Confrontation*, which was aired by the Jamaica Broadcasting Corporation, and the groundbreaking poetry collection *Echo*. Onuora's most recent collection of poetry is *Fuel for Fire*. His albums include *Bus Out, Pressure Drop, Dubbing Away, New Jerusalem Dub, Overdub: A Tribute to King Tubby*, and *I a Tell . . . Dubwise & Otherwise*.

GREGORY PARDLO's debut poetry collection, *Totem*, won the *American Poetry Review*/Honickman First Book Prize in 2007. His poems, reviews, and translations have appeared in *American Poetry Review, Callaloo, Gulf Coast, Harvard Review, Ploughshares*, and on National Public Radio and other radio programs. A finalist for the *Essence* Magazine Literary Award in poetry, he is recipient of a New York Foundation for the Arts Fellowship and a translation grant from the National Endowment for the Arts. He has received other fellowships from the *New York Times*, the MacDowell Colony, the Lotos Club Foundation, and Cave Canem. Pardlo is assistant professor of creative writing at George Washington University and divides his time between Brooklyn, NY, and Washington, DC.

WILLIE PERDOMO is the author *Where a Nickel Costs a Dime* and *Smoking Lovely*, which received a PEN/Beyond Margins Award. He has also been published in the *New York Times Magazine, BOMB, African Voices*, and *CENTRO*. His children's book *Visiting Langston* received a Coretta Scott King Honor. He has been a Pushcart Prize nominee, a Woolrich Fellow in Creative Writing at Columbia University, and was a 2009 New York Foundation for the Arts Poetry Fellow. He is also the cofounder and publisher of Cypher Books. For more information, visit www.willieperdomo.com.

ESTHER PHILLIPS has been anthologized in *The Whistling Bird: Women Writers of the Caribbean* and *Stories from Blue Latitudes: Caribbean Women Writers at Home and Abroad*. Her other works include *When Ground Doves Fly* and *The Stone Gatherer*. She is the head of the division of liberal arts at the Barbados Community College, the founder of Writers Ink Barbados, and the editor of the literary journal *BIM: Arts for the 21st Century*.

GEOFFREY PHILP is the author of the children's book *Grandpa Sydney's Anancy Stories*; a novel, *Benjamin, My Son*; two collections of short stories, *Uncle Obadiah and the Alien* and *Who's Your Daddy? and Other Stories*; and five poetry collections, *Exodus and Other Poems, Florida Bound, Hurricane Center, Xango Music*, and *Twelve Poems and a Story for Christmas*. He lives in Miami, Florida, and is a professor at Miami Dade College.

ROBERT PINSKY's most recent book of poetry is *Gulf Music*. Earlier works include *The Figured Wheel*, awarded the Lenore Marshall Prize, and *The Inferno of Dante*, which won the Howard Morton Landon Translation Award as well as the *Los Angeles Times* Book Prize. His prose works include *The Life of David*, an account of the Biblical hero, and the recent *Thousands of Broadways: Dreams and Nightmares of the American Small Town*. As Poet Laureate of the United States, Pinsky founded the Favorite Poem Project. The recent FPP anthology, *An Invitation to Poetry*, includes a DVD with videos of Americans reading and talking about beloved poems. Pinsky's works about poetry include *The Sounds of Poetry* and *Democracy, Culture and the Voice* *of Poetry.* Pinsky is the only member of the American Academy of Arts and Letters to have appeared on both *The Simpsons* and *The Colbert Report.*

VELMA POLLARD has published poems and stories in regional and international journals and anthologies. She is the author of a novel, two collections of short fiction, two works of nonfiction, a handbook, a monograph, and four books of poetry, including her most recent collection *Leaving Traces.* Her novella *Karl* won the Casa de las Américas Prize in 1992; she was also awarded a Silver Musgrave Medal in 2006. Pollard is a retired senior lecturer in language education at the University of the West Indies, Mona. Her major research interests have been the Creole languages of the Anglophone Caribbean, the language of Caribbean literature, and Caribbean women's writing.

LYNNE PROCOPE describes herself as "a third world poet writing at the jagged rim of the first world." Procope, a teaching artist and poet from Trinidad and Tobago, is a cofounder of the Louder Arts Collective in New York where she directs the Word Shop Series, a biweekly community workshop for developing writers. A member of New York's 1997 National Slam Championship team, she is coauthor of the poetry collection *Burning Down the House.* She has toured and performed across the United States.

CLAUDIA RANKINE was born in Kingston, Jamaica. She is the author of four collections of poetry, *Don't Let Me Be Lonely, PLOT, The End of the Alphabet,* and *Nothing in Nature Is Private,* along with the play *The Provenance of Beauty: A South Bronx Travelogue,* produced in collaboration with the Foundry Theatre. She is also coeditor of *American Women Poets in the Twenty-First Century: Where Lyric Meets Language* and *American Poets in the Twenty-First Century: The New Poetics.* A recipient of fellowships from the Academy of American Poetry, the National Endowment for the Arts, and the Lannan Foundation, Rankine is the Henry G. Lee Professor of English at Pomona College.

KIM ROBINSON-WALCOTT is editor of books and special publications at the Sir Arthur Lewis Institute of Social and Economic Studies, University of the West Indies, Mona. She is also the editor of *Jamaica Journal,* published by the Institute of Jamaica. Her publications include *Out of Order! Anthony Winkler and White West Indian Writing, Jamaican Art,* which she coauthored, and the children's book *Dale's Mango Tree,* which she also illustrated. Her scholarly articles and short stories have been published in a number of journals and anthologies.

CARL HANCOCK RUX has been anthologized as a poet, playwright, fiction writer, and essayist. He is the author of the poetry collection *Pagan Operetta,* which won the *Village Voice Literary Supplement* Prize, and the Obie Award–winning play *Talk.* His critically acclaimed record *Rux Revue* was voted one of the top ten alternative music albums of 1998 by the *New York Times.* Selected by the *New York Times Magazine* as "One of Thirty Artists Under the Age of Thirty Most Likely to Influence Culture Over the Next Thirty Years," and featured on the cover of the *Village Voice* as one of "Eight Writers on the Verge of (Impacting) the Literary Landscape," Rux crosses the disciplines of poetry, theater, music, and literary fiction. Upcoming projects include the release of his sophomore recording project, *Apothecary: Rx,* and the publication of his debut novel *Asphalt*. Rux's honors include the 2002 New York Foundation for the Arts Prize, the 2002 New York Foundation for the Arts Gregory Millard Fellowship, and the Bessie Schomburg award.

SAFFRON, born Phillippa Sauterel, is a Jamaican poet, porcelain artist, and marketing graduate. She has performed her poetry regularly at Harry's Bar and at the Red Bones Blues Café in Kingston. She was featured as a special guest poet at the Poetry Society of Jamaica's fellowship in September 2001, and has appeared on the television programs *Jamaica Magazine* and *Lyrically Speaking*. Her work has been published in the *Sunday Observer*, and the anthologies *Bearing Witness 2 & 3*. Her first collection of poetry, *Soft Flesh*, was published in the 2005 Calabash chapbook series.

KALAMU YA SALAAM, born in 1947, is a poet, author, and teacher from the Ninth Ward of New Orleans. Salaam is codirector of Students at the Center, an independent writing program in the New Orleans public schools. His latest book is the anthology *Ways of Laughing*, and his most recent spoken word album is *Munich Music*. He is the recipient of a 1999 Senior Literature Fellowship from the Fine Arts Work Center in Provincetown, Massachusetts; a 1995 Louisiana Literature Fellow; and guest editor of "The Music" special issue of the *African American Review*. He is moderator of the music website Breath of Life (http://www.kalamu.com/bol) and moderator of e-drum, a listserv for black writers (http://groups.yahoo.com/group/kalamu).

SONIA SANCHEZ is the Poetry Society of America's Robert Frost Medalist for 2001. She is the author of over sixteen books including *Homecoming, We a BaddDDD People, I've Been a Woman: New and Selected Poems, A Sound Investment and Other Stories, Homegirls and Handgrenades, Under a Soprano Sky, Wounded in the House of a Friend, Does Your House Have Lions?, Like the Singing Coming off the Drums*, and, most recently, *Shake Loose My Skin*. Among Sanchez's honors are the 2009 Robert Creeley Poetry Award, a National Endowment for the Arts Fellowship, the Lucretia Mott Award for 1984, the Community Service Award from the National Black Caucus of State Legislators, the 1985 American Book Award for *Homegirls and Handgrenades*, the Governor's Award for Excellence in the Humanities for 1988, a Pew Fellowship in the Arts for 1992–1993, and the Langston Hughes Poetry Award for 1999. *Does Your House Have Lions?* was a finalist for the National Book Critics Circle Award.

ALECIA SAWYERS, a fellow of the Calabash Writer's Workshop, was born and raised in Kingston, Jamaica, and received a BS in counseling psychology at the Mico University. She has been an educator for eighteen years. Her poems have appeared in the *Jamaica Gleaner*.

TIM SEIBLES, born in Philadelphia in 1955, is an American poet and professor. He is the author of five collections of poetry including, most recently, *Buffalo Head Solos*. His honors include an Open Voice Award and fellowships from the National Endowment for the Arts and the Provincetown Fine Arts Work Center. His poems have been published in literary journals and magazines including *Callaloo*, the *Kenyon Review, Indiana Review, Ploughshares, New Letters, Rattle*, and in many anthologies. Seibles earned his BA from Southern Methodist University in 1977. He remained in Dallas after graduating and taught high school English for ten years. He received his MFA from Vermont College in 1990. He is a professor of English and creative writing at Old Dominion University, as well as a visiting faculty member of the Stonecoast MFA Program in Creative Writing. He has taught workshops for Cave Canem and the Hurston/Wright Foundation. He lives in Norfolk, Virginia.

OLIVE SENIOR is the award-winning author of four books of poetry, three books of fiction, and four nonfiction books on Caribbean culture including the *Encyclopedia of Jamaican Heritage* and *Working Miracles: Women's Lives in the English-Speaking Caribbean*. Her short story collections include *Summer Lightning*, winner of the Commonwealth Writers' Prize, *Arrival of the Snake-Woman*, and *Discerner of Hearts*. Her poetry books include *Talking of Trees, Gardening in the Tropics*, winner of the F.J. Bressani Literary Prize, *Over the Roofs of the World*, a finalist for Canada's Governor General's Award and Cuba's Casa de la Américas Prize, and *Shell*, finalist for the Pat Lowther Award. She is the recipient of many other fellowships and awards including the Gold Medal of the Institute of Jamaica.

TANYA SHIRLEY lives in her native Jamaica. She was awarded an MFA in creative writing from the University of Maryland, and is a graduate student and teacher in the Department of Literatures at the University of the West Indies, Mona. Her work has appeared in *Small Axe*, the *Caribbean Writer*, and in *New Caribbean Poetry: An Anthology*. She is a Cave Canem Fellow and a past participant in *Callaloo* creative writing workshops. Her first book of poems, *She Who Sleeps with Bones*, was published in 2009.

ADZIKO SIMBA, of mixed Nigerian and Jamaican heritage, is a writer, performer, storyteller, and workshop facilitator whose writing reflects a Pan-African perspective. Her work has received awards from the Jamaica Cultural Development Commission, the Commonwealth Broadcasting Association, Montserrat's National St. Patrick's Day Literary Competition, and the *Observer* literary arts magazine. Simba has written for BBC television and Jamaican radio. She has cowritten five stage plays and is currently at work on a novel.

LOUIS SIMPSON was born in Jamaica in 1923, the son of a lawyer of Scottish descent and a Russian mother. He emigrated to the United States at the age of seventeen, studied at Columbia University, then served in the Second World War with the 101st Airborne Division on active duty in France, Holland, Belgium, and Germany. After the war he continued his studies at Columbia and the University of Paris. While living in France he published his first book of poems, *The Arrivistes*. He worked as an editor in a publishing house in New York, then earned a PhD at Columbia and went on to teach at Columbia, the University of California, Berkeley, and the State University of New York, Stony Brook. Simpson has published eighteen volumes of poetry including *At the End of the Open Road*, for which he was awarded the Pulitzer Prize in 1964. He has also published a novel, an autobiography, memoirs, and literary criticism. His most recent books are *The Owner of the House: New Collected Poems (1940-2001)* and *Struggling Times*.

PATRICIA SMITH is the author of five books of poetry including *Blood Dazzler*, chronicling the tragedy of Hurricane Katrina, which was a finalist for the 2008 National Book Award, one of *Library Journal*'s Best Poetry Books of 2008, and one of NPR's top five books of 2008; and *Teahouse of the Almighty*, a National Poetry Series selection, winner of the Hurston/Wright Legacy Award, and About.com's Best Poetry Book of 2006. She also authored the groundbreaking history *Africans in America* and the award-winning children's book *Janna and the Kings*. Her work, which she has performed around the world, has appeared in *Poetry*, the *Paris Review*, *TriQuarterly*, and many other journals. She is a Pushcart Prize winner and a four-time individual champion of the National Poetry Slam, the most successful poet in the competition's history. She is a professor at the College of Staten Island, City University of New York, and is on the faculty of both Cave Canem and the Stonecoast MFA program at the University of Southern Maine. For more information, visit www.wordwoman.ws.

DEANNE SOARES is a lecturer in the faculty of medical sciences at the University of the West Indies. She is a Calabash Writer's Workshop alumna and has been published online at Strategy, Forethought, and Insight.

TANYA STEPHENS is a reggae artist whose most recent album is *Rebelution*, following the huge success of *Gangsta Blues*. Her recording career began in 1993 with the release of the single "Is This for Real." Her first hit came a year later in 1994 with the single "Big Tings a Gwaan." Other hits since then include "Goggle," "Yuh Nuh Ready," and "It's a Pity." Considered by many to be one of the most literary writers in the history of the deejay profession, her work has received critical acclaim in major media outlets, including the *New York Times*, *Village Voice*, *Vibe*, and the *Source*.

ANDREW STONE was born in Kingston, Jamaica, where he still resides. He is a graduate of the University of the West Indies. His poetry appears regularly in Jamaican newspapers. His first collection of poetry, *In Disguise,* was published in the 2005 Calabash chapbook series.

TERESE SVOBODA has published eleven books of prose and poetry including, most recently, *Weapons Grade*. Her honors include the Graywolf Nonfiction Prize, an O. Henry Prize for short fiction, a Pushcart Prize for nonfiction, a Jerome Foundation grant in video, the John Golden Award in playwriting, the Bobst Prize in fiction, and the Iowa Prize in poetry. She lives in New York City and often writes about the south Sudanese, the Cook Islanders, and African American soldiers in postwar Japan.

EVERTON SYLVESTER, poet and screenwriter, is the author of *Backyard in Bed-Stuy*. He was a 1993 James Michener Fellow and a 1997 and 1998 Sundance Screenwriters Lab Fellow. His screenplay *Tambourine* was a top-five finalist in the 2002 Urban World Film Festival. Sylvester performs with the Brooklyn Funk Essentials band as well as his acoustic quartet Searching for Banjo. He lives in Brooklyn, New York. When he's not touring, he restores brownstone buildings.

FABIAN THOMAS is an actor, director, poet, writer, singer, communications consultant, trainer/facilitator, and HIV/AIDS educator, with over twenty-five years of experience in the performing arts. His theatrical directorial credits include *Dreamgirls*, *VOICES, VOICES: Unoo Nuh Hear Dem?, 'night Mother, Di Fallen Angel an Di Devil's Concubine, Grease,* Aston Cooke's *Jamaican Pepperpot* and *Concubine,* and Trevor Rhone's musical edu-drama *POSITIVE*. He has been nominated for several ITI Jamaica Actor Boy Awards and has won the prize once. Thomas is a Calabash Writer's Workshop Fellow and is currently working on his first book of poetry.

RALPH THOMPSON has published poems in British, American, and Caribbean journals including the *Caribbean Writer* and the *Mississippi Review*. His work is represented in *The Heinemann Book of Caribbean Poetry*, *A World of Poetry for CXC*, several *Observer* arts magazine anthologies, *The Oxford Book of Caribbean Verse*, and *Writers Who Paint/Painters Who Write*. He has published two collections of poetry, *The Denting of a Wave* and *Moving On*, and a verse novel, *View from Mount Diablo*, which won the Jamaican National Literary Prize for manuscript in 2001.

NATASHA TRETHEWEY is the author of *Native Guard*, for which she won the 2007 Pulitzer Prize, *Bellocq's Ophelia*, which was named a Notable Book for 2003 by the American Library Association, and *Domestic Work*. She is the recipient of fellowships from the Guggenheim Foundation, the Rockefeller Foundation Bellagio Study Center, the National Endowment for the Arts, and the Bunting Fellowship Program of the Radcliffe Institute for Advanced Study at Harvard. Her poems have appeared in journals and anthologies including *American Poetry Review*, *Callaloo*, *Kenyon Review*, the *Southern Review*, *New England Review*, *Gettysburg Review*, and several volumes of *The Best American Poetry*. Currently, she is a professor of English and holds the Phillis Wheatley Distinguished Chair in Poetry at Emory University.

DEREK WALCOTT, winner of the 1992 Nobel Prize in Literature, was born in 1930 in St. Lucia. He has published five books of plays and eleven books of poetry. His many honors and awards include an Obie Award for the play *Dream On Monkey Mountain*, the Guinness Award for Poetry, a Royal Society of Literature Award, the Cholmondeley Prize, the *New Statesman*'s Jock Campbell Award, the Arts Council of Wales International Writers Prize, a five-year fellowship from the MacArthur Foundation, and the Queen's Medal for Poetry. His recent works include *Selected Poems*, published in 2007 and edited by Edward Baugh, and *White Egrets*. Walcott divides his time between his homes in St. Lucia and New York and his numerous speaking and teaching engagements worldwide.

AFAA MICHAEL WEAVER, born Michael S. Weaver, is a veteran of fifteen years as a blue-collar factory worker in his native Baltimore. He received a BA from Regents College and an MFA from Brown University. His books of poetry include *Multitudes: Poems Selected & New*, *The Ten Lights of God*, *Sandy Point*, and an anthology, *These Hands I Know: African-American Writers on Family*. His tenth and newest collection is *The Plum Flower Dance: Poems 1985 to 2005*. He received a National Endowment for the Arts Fellowship in 1985 and a fellowship from the Pew Charitable Trusts in 1998. In 2002, he was a Fulbright Visiting Scholar at National Taiwan University and Taipei National University of the Arts. He holds an endowed chair at Simmons College in Boston, where he is alumnae professor of English. Also a playwright and short-fiction writer, Weaver has received a Pushcart Prize and the May Sarton Award. For more information, visit www.afaamweaver.com.

DANIEL WIDEMAN is coeditor of *Soulfires: Young Black Men on Love and Violence*. His work has been widely anthologized in journals and books including *Giant Steps: The New Generation of African-American Writers*, *Step into a World: A Global Anthology of the New Black Literature*, *Outside the Law: Narratives of Justice in America*, and *Commonwealth: Contemporary Poets on Pennsylvania*.

PERMISSIONS